IMAGES
of America

ADIRONDACK
HOTELS AND INNS

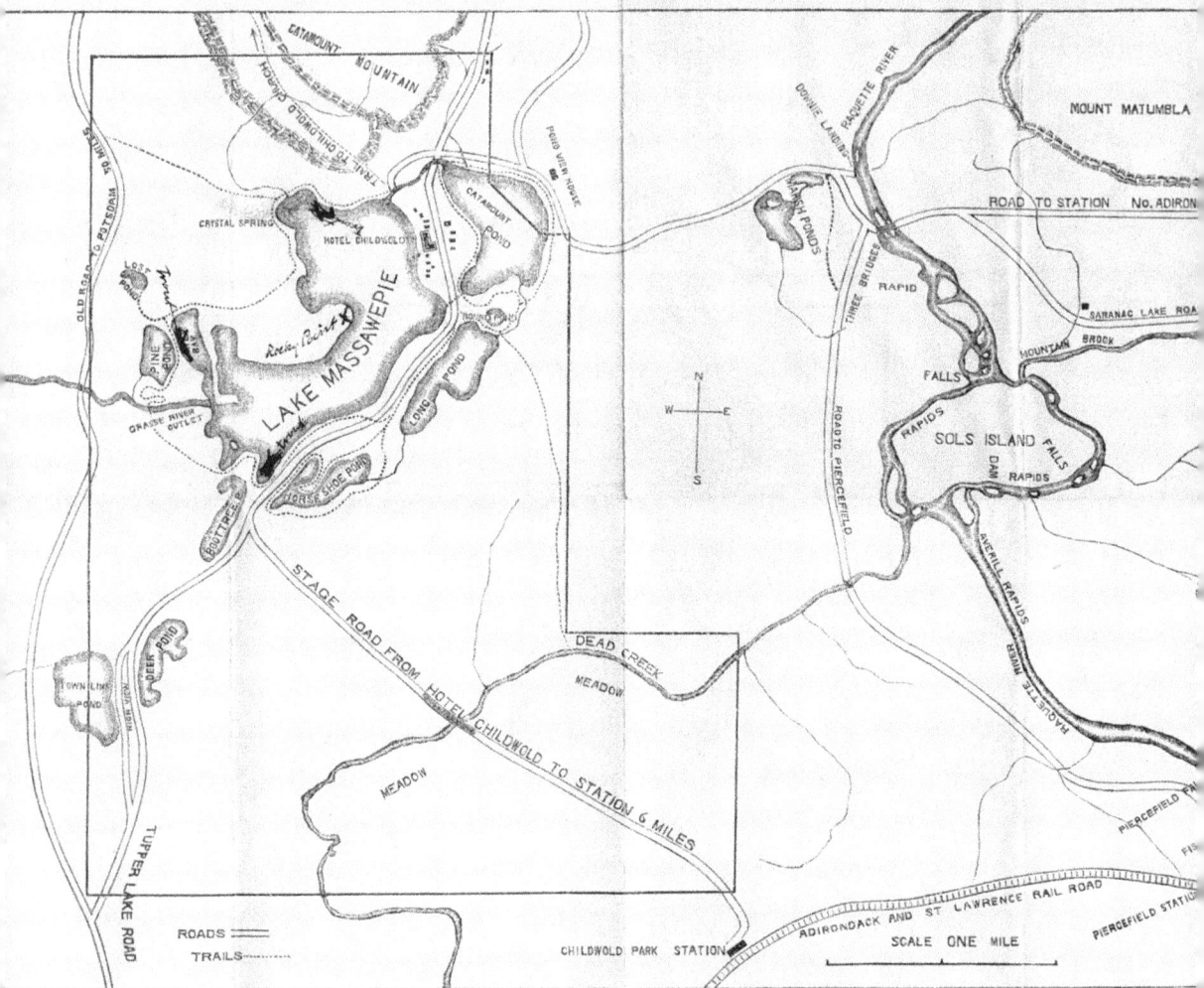

CHILDWOLD PARK

By the end of the 1880s, the Adirondacks had become the place to be for vacations. People wanted to experience the Adirondack offerings, and hotels often included well-kept grounds and parks around their hostelries. Childwold, near Tupper Lake, maintained a park that was more than seven square miles on its property along with hiking trails and waters. Note the three trout fishing locations marked on Lake Massawepie; fishing attracted many to the Adirondack hotels.

On the cover: The Hosley House in Wells, Hamilton County, was built in 1899 by Martin B. and John G. Hosley to offer accommodations to those entering the Adirondacks from the south. Passengers who disembarked at the Fonda, Johnstown and Gloversville Railroad (FJ&G) terminus at Northville boarded the stagecoach to travel to their Adirondack destinations. The Hosley House became a regular stop on the coach line. The hotel changed ownership over the years and was known as Zeiser's Hotel Wells, the Riley House, and Hunt's Hotel. One of the last remaining of the original Adirondack hotels, the Hosley House is now being restored to its original splendor and operates as a rehabilitation center. (Author's collection.)

IMAGES
of America

ADIRONDACK HOTELS AND INNS

Donald R. Williams

ARCADIA
PUBLISHING

Published by Arcadia Publishing
Charleston, South Carolina

Library of Congress Catalog Card Number: 2007935870

For all general information contact Arcadia Publishing at:
Telephone 843-853-2070
Fax 843-853-0044
E-mail sales@arcadiapublishing.com
For customer service and orders:
Toll-Free 1-888-313-2665

Visit us on the Internet at www.arcadiapublishing.com

To Adirondack writers, past and present, who flesh out those vivifying stories of the Adirondack people and places and raise them up to be enjoyed by many for years to come.

CONTENTS

ACKNOWLEDGMENTS

The previous four books in the Images of America series that I wrote for Arcadia Publishing are a tribute to those who shared their memories of and photographs from the Adirondacks. Fleshing out the stories and photographs is an endless job, and it takes a major commitment to complete a book. Without a lifetime collection of Adirondackia, family archives, and the support of family and friends, no book would reach fulfillment. Thank you to those who made *Adirondack Hotels and Inns* possible.

INTRODUCTION

The Adirondack region of New York State enjoyed a hotel era that lasted some 100 years, from 1850 to 1950. Hostelries, a term that has fallen into disuse with today's motels and resorts, included all the Adirondack accommodations, such as boardinghouses, camps, cabins, tents, hotels, inns, farmhouses, lodges, tourist homes, and guesthouses. They dominated the Adirondack scene in the heyday of 1850–1950, providing bed and board for the thousands who enjoyed a sojourn in the forested region.

In my estimation, some 1,000 hotels and hundreds of other hostelries were serving the needs of the traveling public during the hotel era. Some evidence exists that indicates that before 1875, there were over 200 hotels in the Adirondacks. At one time, Hamilton County alone had over 250 hotels. In the days following the Civil War, Americans developed an interest in travel throughout their now united lands. Trains, steamers, and stagecoaches came into widespread use to help the travelers reach their Adirondack destinations.

Penetrating the Adirondacks for vacation was promoted at several points. Early publications, such as D. Appleton Publishing Company's 1890 *Handbook of American Travel*, promoting travel to the Adirondacks, "a wilderness the size of Connecticut," suggested a route into the Chateaugay Woods that led from Plattsburgh to Dannemora and Chazy Lake or from Rouse's Point to Chateaugay four corners and Chazy Lake. Another route led into the Saranac Region by Lake Champlain steamboat and post coach to Keeseville. From Keeseville, the stage took passengers to Baker's Saranac Lake House and to Martin's on Lower Saranac. A good plank road was built from Keeseville, 30 miles to Franklin Falls. Another Adirondack route led to the Hudson River and Raquette Lake regions. A stagecoach trip from Crown Point on Lake Champlain went 20 miles to Roots and on to the MacIntyre Mine site. Travelers could go to Scott's on the Elizabethtown Road, "through the woods with scarcely a path," and on to Baker's Boarding House. Adirondack travelers would also enter the Adirondacks at Glens Falls, Carthage, Fort Edward, Northville, or "by road from Saratoga to Lake Pleasant and Piseco."

In the 1880s, tourists were also told to take the railroad or boat up the picturesque Hudson River to Albany. A new iron boat, *City of Albany*, was the fastest-running boat ever on the New York-Albany line. The Delaware and Hudson Railroad was boarded at Albany and went past the largely known camp meeting resort Round Lake to Saratoga. Fort Edward was the next stop where passengers could get off for Lake George or stay on to Ticonderoga. At Ti, the steamer *Horicon* would take passengers the length of Lake George to Caldwell. Others took the steamer *Vermont* to Port Kent to get the Harper Stage over the plank road to Ausable Chasm. Philadelphians could leave after dinner and reach the chasm for breakfast the next day. Travel to the Adirondacks a hundred years ago was not as easy as jumping in the car today, but it may have been more adventurous and possibly less stressful.

Once the sojourners reached the Adirondacks, what did they find? In the beginning of the hotel era, accommodations were somewhat scarce. When the Reverend W. H. H. "Adirondack" Murray wrote his Adirondack travel book in 1869, he enticed thousands to seek out the health-giving features and recreation found in the Adirondacks. He described the Adirondack hotels as ostentatious, having good reputations, well-deserved, offering solid comfort, and having appointments that were thorough and complete. He praised the hotelkeepers for their congenial manners. Unfortunately, there were not enough hotels to accommodate "Murray's rush."

Hostelries multiplied and by the 1900s, Adirondack accommodations included the deluxe resorts where every wish was anticipated; the hotel where one vacations among homey surroundings offering planned entertainment; the mountain lodge, or chalet, where life was informal; the quaint inns for relaxation; the housekeeping cottages, tourist homes, boardinghouses, farmhouses, and guesthouses with modest prices; the dude ranches where fun is king; the children's camps with special programs; and the hunting camps and tent sites for roughing it.

During the hotel era in the Adirondacks, the hotels and inns were springing up in the mountain region of New York State like the springtime dandelions on your lawn. Most had a series of owners. They were financed and managed locally and hired local help. Some had visitors from all over America, the famous and the not so famous. Most advertised trout and venison dinners. They employed Adirondack guides. Virtually all were built of wood and, unfortunately, could not survive a fire and the changing tastes of the American public.

There were a variety of reasons why Americans came to the Adirondack region of New York State. In the beginning of major human intrusion, it was for trapping and hunting. Logging and tanning caused an influx, and then the settlers multiplied. Artists and writers found the Adirondacks. Others, hearing of the good fishing and hunting and learning of the sparkling lakes and mountain trails and the health-giving features of the Adirondacks, persuaded local settlers to rent rooms so they could spend time in the pleasant climate of the mountain region. The rest is history; hostelries grew and spread to provide accommodations for the thousands who found reasons to enjoy Adirondack country.

Once people found the Adirondacks, the forested mountain trails and dirt roadways evolved into major highways that crisscrossed the region. Gateway towns and cities grew up to provide on-the-route accommodations and an entranceway to the Adirondack roadways. Today they have become official byways and include the Adirondack Trail (Route 30A-30), the Central Adirondack Trail (Route 28), the Olympic Trail (Route 3), the Roosevelt-Marcy Trail (Route 28N), the Dude Ranch Trail (Route 9N, 28), the High Peaks Byway (Route 73), the Blue Ridge Road (Route 2B), the Southern Adirondack Trail (Route 8), the Lakes to Locks Passage, and the Colonial Trail (Route 9N). Hotels, inns, and other hostelries were built along these major routes, which made it possible for travelers to reach their accommodations without undue hardships, whether by stagecoach or later automobiles. Mail and delivery routes were also able to provide their services to the mountain country settlements. Good access roads became important to the hostelries and others who offered Adirondack accommodations.

In 1927, summer boys' camp director Lawrence F. Fountain, son of Adirondack hotelkeepers Lee and Ott Fountain, wrote his master thesis on the "Human Geography of the Upper Sacandaga Valley." He foresaw the changeover from dependence on lumbering and limited agriculture to the emerging tourism. He concluded, "we see that increasing industrialization of the United States and the tremendous growth of our cities in recent years have caused the forest regions nearby to have a new value, an esthetic value, which yield handsome returns if properly exploited." And so the people came, and so did the hostelries.

One

Adirondack Trail
Hostelries

The Jackson House at Mayfield, at the gateway of the Adirondack Trail, is the scene of those traveling in the Adirondacks before the automobile days. Stagecoaches, farm wagons, surreys, freight wagons, and other horse-drawn and ox-drawn vehicles made early use of the Adirondack Trail as it connected the developing settlements. Hotel keeping became a major industry on the trail to handle the influx of travelers who had to spend the night or stay for business or pleasure.

The Adirondack Inn, built in 1890 at Sacandaga Park, was advertised as the "Adirondack–Gem of the North" by the Fonda, Johnstown and Gloversville Railroad. In 1937, a 23-room addition brought it up to 160 guest rooms with everything "modern and for comfort." It boasted easy access to the railroad, dancing every evening, a post office and a telegraph office in house, and the New York papers daily. Along with this, the inn offered "beautiful and primitive scenery, rest, recreation and health" in its 1895 brochure, *Sacandaga Park*. Concerts were held on the lawn of the Adirondack Inn and in an adjacent bandstand. The John Philip Sousa Band and E. W. Prouty's Military Band and Orchestra of Boston brought top-quality music to the park. Dance bands performed in the ballroom at the Adirondack Inn, and an open-air pavilion offered free dancing on Saturday evenings.

Hotel Pines in the Adirondacks, Sacandaga Park, New York. Stanton Bogaskie, Prop.

The Hotel Pines, on the banks of the Sacandaga River at Sacandaga Park, was only a five-minute walk from the railroad station. Many hotels were built on the rail lines to take advantage of the transportation and the advertising done by the railroad companies. The Pines restaurant offered a daily menu, complete with major entrées and fancy desserts. In its bar and café it carried all the popular brands of whiskey as well as beer on draught for 10¢ per glass. It was one of the few hotels that had its own skating rink. Stanton Bogaskie was the proprietor and announced it was opening by Memorial Day each year. Other hostelries in the park included the Osborne Inn, Log Cabin Inn, Corbett Cottage, and Allens Cottage.

The Old Orchard Inn stood on the sharp corner and the southern exit from Sacandaga Park, conveniently situated on the border to the historic Sacandaga Park Golf Course. Opened on March 5, 1913, the three-story inn was under the proprietorship of C. H. Osborne, a well-known Adirondack hotel operator. The Old Orchard Inn was demolished in 1965, and only a vacant lot remains today.

The construction date of the St. James Hotel between Sacandaga Park and Northville is unknown, but the vehicle in the photograph, an early bus loaded with passengers going to the park, indicates that it was at the beginning of the 20th century. Some evidence exists that it was operating as a hotel before World War I.

12

High Rock Lodge owed its popularity to the Sacandaga Amusement Park, the "Coney Island of the Adirondacks." Built on a hillside overlooking the park, it attracted hikers, tourists, parkgoers, and entertainers over its 50-year history. The lodge, operating as a farmhouse inn, was built in 1901 by James Hull for Reuben D. Buckingham. The large rock pictured here, located on the site, became a popular hiking destination for the thousands who came to enjoy the Sacandaga Park attractions. In 1940, Ashley and Mildred Dawes purchased the three-story, 54-room hostelry and operated it as a summer lodge and cottages, along with a restaurant. It burned on August 22, 1951. After the fire, Mildred continued the hostelry, converting her house on the property into a dining room and cocktail lounge. Lodging continued in the several cottages on the property.

A New York State historic marker near the Northville Bridge on the Adirondack Trail, Route 30 marks the terminus of the railroad line that brought vacationers and others to the southern gateway of the Adirondacks. Once the Fonda, Johnstown and Gloversville Railroad (FJ&G) was connected to the New York Central Railroad at Fonda in 1870, the need of a spur to Northville was evident. The Northville and Gloversville Railroad Company was formed with $20,000 in bonds, along with a stock company of $200,000. The finances did not work, so the line was sold to the FJ&G. From 1875 to 1930, those who stayed in the southern Adirondack hostelries in Northville, Hope, Wells, Speculator, Lake Pleasant, Piseco, and other internal Adirondack places took the train to Northville and then, in the early years, boarded the stagecoaches and horse-drawn hacks and later took Model-T Ford taxis and autobuses to their destinations.

The Northville House, or Hotel Northville, was built in 1813 by Abraham Van Arnam for his daughter and her husband, James Lobdell. Abraham's brother, Jacob Van Arnam, later became the owner and converted the home into a hotel. A portion of the hotel was burned in a fire in 1898, and it was repaired. The 138-year-old hotel ceased operation in 1951 with Alfred Sawyer, who ran it for 10 years, as the last proprietor. Hiram Denton and Claude Lipe, proprietors of a small furniture store since 1947, purchased the large building for their growing furniture business. In 1960, Milton Groff, who had been associated with the business since 1949, became the owner of the firm. In 1999, the Northville House was purchased from James Groff by Pat and Kevin Richard, with the idea of restoring it to its former grandeur by its 200th birthday in 2013.

The Winney House, Northville, N.Y.

Gardner Winney built the Sacandaga Hotel at the foot of Prospect Hill in Northville in 1867 and lost it to fire in 1888. An 1882 advertisement in the Northville *Tri-Weekly Herald* had called the Reed Street hotel the Sacandaga House, with G. Winney as the proprietor. At the time of the fire, a family wedding was taking place in the nearby Duncan home. Charles Duncan, brother of the bride, ran to fight the fire in his wedding clothes. Winney built a second hotel on the South Main Street site of another hotel, the National, and operated it until it also partially succumbed to fire. Today the remaining front portion of the building has been moved to South Second Street and made into a two-family house. The original Winney House barn is being used for the Red Barn Collectible and Gift Shop.

NORTH MAIN STREET, ANIBAL HOUSE, NORTHVILLE, N. Y.

The "Towers," as it was known, was built around 1870 on the west side of North Main Street in Northville. It began as a livery and boarding stable, owned and operated by W. H. Grennell. Later it was made into a two-and-a-half-story hotel. The Tower Inn had several owners over the years and several name changes, including the Anibal House, Kathans, Flewellings, Tunnicliffs, and the Avalon. John Willard once owned the property. It was the Anibal House with Leon R. Anibal, proprietor, in 1895 when it became the site of the arrest of a U. S. Army deserter, James "Klocky" Cowles, by Gloversville deputy sheriff Getman. It became known as the Avalon when it was run by L. F. Yager. Henry Flewelling renamed it Tunnicliffs in 1926. Franklin Wadsworth was the last owner, and the Tower Inn burned down in 1958.

STATEMENT

Northville, N. Y., *May 14* 190 9

M. B. Hurley

In Account with **ANIBAL HOUSE**

LEON R. ANIBAL, PROPRIETOR

(FORMERLY OF HOTEL WINNEY)

MS CASH   FIRST CLASS LIVERY CONNECTED

To Bird
Livry   ·65 50
                                    54 00
                                   119 50

The above account is past due. Not hearing from you before the
................., will draw on you.

17

Northville, once known as the "gateway to the Adirondack lumbering business," became a stopping-off point for those working on the winter logging jobs. The terminus of the railroad brought thousands and created a demand for food and lodging. Along with the loggers came the hunters, the tourists, and the business travelers. The Lyon House, one of the original 13 Northville hotels, was once the Arlington Hotel and the Dopp House.

Tent camps were found throughout the mountains. Religious revivals, such as those held near Northville on the Sacandaga River, used tents for accommodations. Some hotels used tents to add to their availability of beds. Some of the tuberculosis patients who came to the Adirondacks seeking a cure were placed in sleeping tents. Those with better means often decorated their tents with carpets, full-size beds, plants, and washing facilities.

18

Arnolds Boat Livery and Cabins, overlooking the Great Sacandaga Lake at Giffords Valley near Northville, consisted of four cabins along with a boathouse building and dock. The business, owned by Floyd and Mable Arnold, opened after the flooding of the Sacandaga Valley with the construction of the dam for the Sacandaga Reservoir, later named the Great Sacandaga Lake. Two additional cabins were brought in after the business became better known. Families who came, year after year, to stay in the cabins enjoyed some of the Adirondack agricultural experiences. They selected, picked, and purchased sweet corn from the adjacent Williams family farm, along with other seasonal vegetables. And they had their own private privy in a four-room outhouse, each with two holes. In connection with the cabins, patrons could rent boats at the boat livery and purchase other fishing needs and snacks.

Kennyetto Inn, Broadalbin, N. Y.

HOTEL BROADALBIN
Lunch · Fine Dining · Spirits
BANQUET FACILITIES

HOTEL BROADALBIN

Built in 1854 of brick to house the Northrup and Richardson Glove Company, this building was purchased in 1881 by Charles W. Bass, who operated it as the Kennyetto Hotel, the largest hotel in the county at the time. In 1899, it became a medical center with a surgeon and an alcohol treatment center. By 1904, the building served as a hotel again by owner Mr. Farley. It changed hands in 1908 to Wilber S. Thom and again in 1911 to Frederick W. Crosswait. Steve Kross, noted restaurateur, bought it in 1924. The name was changed to Hotel Broadalbin. It was then sold to Joseph and Stanley Wojtowicz in 1968 and finally to John Ulrich in 1973. In 2007, another sale was in the works.

Fish House, originally called Northampton after the patent, took its name from the 1762 sporting lodge built by Sir William Johnson on the banks of the Sacandaga River. The building was burned down during the American Revolution, but the name remained. In March 1961, 95 percent of the town residents voted to make Fish House the official name of the village. The Fish House Hotel was built in 1803, about the time of the first post office. The hotel burned down after Prohibition.

Wadsworth House, Hope, N. Y.
On Sacandaga River Road to Wells, Adirondack Mountains.

William Wadsworth and his wife, Myra, operated a hotel in Hope on the Adirondack Trail from 1891 to 1908 in a building constructed by Josiah Wadsworth Jr. in 1853. Two other buildings were added, the Camp and the Coop, and it became a popular summer boardinghouse. The walls of the building were built of two-inch upright planks with clapboards on the outside and plaster on the inside. Guests came mostly from New York City and Long Island. Ryan, son of the owners, took over the management when the parents retired.

Silas Torrey's Hotel, later Bud Davison's Hotel, served the travelers and lumbermen in the town of Hope. The small building behind the hotel in the winter photograph was the icehouse, a necessary building for most of the pre-electricity Adirondack hotels. Before the building became Torrey's Hotel, it was known as Ostranders. According to superintendent of the state survey Verplanck Colvin's map of 1898, those who left Northville for Wells would pass Frasier's Hotel before the Hamilton County line, J. P. Harris' Hotel before the Stoney Creek Bridge, F. Willard's Hotel just past the Willard Cemetery, Torrey's Hotel on today's town of Hope Fire Department site, the J. Pritchard's Hotel just past Dewey Creek, and Coulombe Hotel at the entrance to the Pumpkin Hollow Road.

In 1882, the small settlement of Ashton had a post office. The original hotel built in 1880 was known as Coulombe's Hotel on early maps and was still operating in 1925 with Sam Preston as hotelkeeper. Adam Cashinsky bought it and renamed the settlement Cashville and the hotel Cashinsky's. In the 1940s, it became Moore's Hotel, owned by Ted Moore and his wife, although some continued to call it the Ashton Hotel. The garage in the photograph is the last remaining remnant of the popular stopping-off place.

The teams of horses in this 1903 photograph illustrate the widespread use of horse-drawn vehicles on the Adirondack Trail before the onset of the automobile. The teams are loading and unloading in front of a hotel in Wells that, at that time, was being run by Frank "Pants" Lawrence. They most likely picked up passengers at the FJ&G station at Northville and traveled to the hotels in Hope and beyond.

Physical Training Farm on Sacandaga River, Northville, N.Y. 453

Oral history told of a unique Adirondack hostelry on the corner of the Adirondack Trail (Route 30) and the Pumpkin Hollow Road near Wells. Some remember a big swimming pool, and others remember a long bowling alley. Groups of men walking along the highway for exercise were observed by local residents. Vintage photographs provide evidence of the once thriving "Physical Training Farm." The 100-acre property included a hotel, a dance hall, a 40-by-60-foot gymnasium, a swimming pool, a bowling alley, and a private pond. The photograph of "Bill's Gym" shows baskets for basketball, tennis racquets, and trapeze rings. The health farm property later became the site of a hotel known over the years as Wilfred Coulombe's hotel, Cashinsky's Hotel when owned by Adam Cashinsky, Moore's Hotel under the ownership of Ted Moore and his wife, and later the Ashton Hotel.

Bill's Gym, 40 x 60, Physical Training Farm, Northville, N.Y. 454

Adirondack Inn, Wells, N. Y.

The Adirondack Inn, one of the most used names for an Adirondack hostelry, began its life as the home of William Welds where he rented rooms. Around 1870, James Mitchell opened the Adirondack Inn on the site. In 1895, Thomas McCann held the mortgage, and Mary Mitchell became the new owner in 1897 with a mortgage from Lee S. Anibal of Northville, who took over the hotel in 1900. Logger John Horey was the proprietor sometime between 1900 and 1905. On November 20, 1909, a news item announced the sale of the Adirondack Inn property located at Wells. Robert Stuart sold the hotel to parties in Troy for $4,500. Shortly after this sale, it became Allen's Hotel with Ruth Allen as proprietor. Other owners included William Cochrane, William Ronald, W. H. Moshier, Frank "Pants" Lawrence, Thomas Vill, and Lee Fountain. The inn burned down in 1929.

Morrison's Boarding House at Wells served sportsmen and the vacationing public for many years. With Lake Algonquin, constructed in 1925, in the foreground and the mountains in the background, it provided an Adirondack setting conducive to a restful vacation. George Morrison operated the boardinghouse until the middle of the 20th century, when it was torn down and replaced with a private home.

Those who traveled to the Adirondacks in the hotel era often stayed for the summer. They would arrange a two-month stay at a boardinghouse or hotel and bring their trunks filled with the necessities for the summer social and outdoor life. Families chose to stay at the same hostelry each year, becoming close friends with the owner, staff, and other vacationers. The group shown here was staying at Hosley's Boarding House in Wells.

Whitehouse in the Adirondacks traces its name back to at least 1899, and the road to the Whitehouse near Wells predates the Civil War times. It was a large, white farmhouse, nine miles over a dirt road in the woods. It became a lodge, hunting camp, and cabins that came down to Lee and Olive "Ott" Fountain in 1925. It was a busy Adirondack hostelry, with the Northville-Lake Pleasant stagecoach making a detour during the summer season to transport passengers to the remote site. At the same time the Fountains ran the Whitehouse business, they had a successful rustic furniture business, making chairs and tables out of the Adirondack yellow birch trees. Lee and Ott turned the business over to their son Lawrence and his wife, Liberty, in 1945. It later sold to Milo Niffen and Edward Richards, who operated it as a hunting preserve until 1956, when it became part of the New York State Forest Preserve.

27

HOTEL COCHRANE, WELLS, N. Y.

William Pettit opened his Wells Hotel in 1863. It soon became the town meeting place, with a meeting in February 1864 to approve a $400 bounty for Civil War volunteers. In 1868, it was used by the town to deal with the smallpox epidemic. The board of supervisors was meeting there by 1877, and the town board met at the hotel in 1886 to discuss raising the covered bridge two feet. In 1890, they met at the hotel to set new election districts in the growing town. It was a common practice to use the Adirondack hostelries in the small settlements as meeting places. In 1895, William's son, Joel, took over for the next 10 years. Martin Kelly owned the hotel for a short time, and in 1905, David Cochrane purchased the business and it became Cochrane's Hotel. The building was torn down in 1929 to provide a site for the Hamilton County National Bank and has now become the municipal building and library.

Restoration work continues on the 40-guest Hosley House in Wells, bringing back the original construction of one of the remaining hostelries of the Adirondacks' heyday. The *Hamilton County Record* newspaper noted on May 3, 1900, that "the office counter and fixtures for the new Hosley House are now in position. The counter is a handsome piece of work and was the product of the Norwood Manufacturing Company." The *Utica Sunday Globe* of June 21, 1919, printed a photograph of a large hotel building with a caption that read, "New Hosley House at Wells, New York, a popular hostelry in the picturesque Adirondack region." The printed article placed elsewhere on the page continued, "The accompanying illustration gives a very good idea of the new Hosley House at Wells, which is now open to the public. The house is 40 by 60 feet and three stories high. It has accommodations for about 50 to 60 people and is up-to-date in its appointments."

Sampson Hosley once ran a hotel next to the location of today's Hunts Hotel, originally the Hosley House. There is some evidence to indicate that once the Hosley House was built in 1898 by M. B. and J. G. Hosley, it became a major stopping point for the stagecoaches and other travelers. The once Samp Hosley's Hotel next door became the Hosley House Annex, catering to the overflow of patrons for the big hotel. Today the building has become part of a private home.

Some Adirondack hostelries were provided by religious groups that offered food, lodging, and programs. Some provided tents, some dormitories, and some hotel-type accommodations. Services and concerts were part of the summer offerings. The Camp-of-the-Woods on Lake Pleasant was founded by YMCA camp director George "Pops" Tibbitts. When he saw Lake Pleasant and the little village of Speculator he decided, as quoted on the jacket of *The Mystery of Kunjumuck Cave* by George Tibbitts, "to build a place where city dwellers could enjoy the beauty and the health-giving qualities of the Adirondacks," the goal of all the Adirondack hostelries.

THE OSBORNE INN, Speculator, N. Y.

[handwritten postcard text, partially legible]

Heavyweight boxer Gene Tunney trained for his bout with world heavyweight champion Jack Dempsey in 1926 at the Osborne Inn at Speculator. He won the title from Dempsey and returned to Speculator in 1928 to train for other fights. Will and Nora Osborne built the Osborne Inn in 1901 on the shore of Lake Pleasant. Will passed away in 1902, and Nora carried on the successful business. Other boxers helped to bring the inn to national prominence before it closed in 1963 and was demolished in 1969.

Bearhurst was built on Lake Pleasant in 1895 by Emil Meyrowitz for a summer home. Today it has evolved into an Adirondack hostelry owned by the Funfschilling family. The main lodge, with its nine rooms, three baths, four massive fireplaces, and large dining room and main hall, along with the cooks and servants' house, icehouse, woodshed, pump house, boathouse, cottage, and garage, provides space for individual guest cottages. The six-sided gazebo and stonework walkways have stood on the lake's shore for over 100 years.

Moving buildings in the Adirondacks was a common occurrence when the population grew and tourism became the major industry. Buildings were moved by sledges, rollers, and sleighs from abandoned tanning villages and camps. Graham's Hotel in Speculator, built in 1923 by DeWitt Graham, was moved from a small side road across the main street to today's location. Over the years, it has served as a hotel, a dance hall, a barbershop, a bar, a restaurant, and a gift shop.

Lee Fountain grew up on East Road in Speculator and made his fortune without going too far from home. Once out of school, he became the district tax collector for Newton's Corner, later Speculator, and took a job at the veneer mill in Wells. With the money he earned, he soon opened a general store in Speculator. His next venture was Lee Fountain's Hotel, near Speculator's four corners. He also began his rustic furniture making in the adjacent barn.

The Sturges House (or Sturges Hotel) stood for some 85 years about 200 feet north of the four corners in Speculator. A Sturges House annex was built for overflow from the hotel, and it still stands across the road from the main building site, providing food and lodging. Shoemaker Aaron Sturges came to Lake Pleasant in 1832 and built a shanty on the banks of Lewey Lake. He became a professional hunter and fisherman, and his two sons, David and James, worked as Adirondack guides. David went on to build the Sturges House in 1858 and owned it for more than 50 years. The Sturges House advertised "an ideal location for a summer hotel." Its rooms for 400 guests were all large and well lit, with a "view that never wearies." They had an excellent chef and owned a large vegetable farm and a fine dairy. Lee and Ott Fountain, experienced Adirondack hotelkeepers, ran the Sturges House in 1907.

"MORLEYS" AND COTTAGES, LAKE PLEASANT, N. Y. ADIRONDACK MOUNTAINS.

Morleys Hotel, at the head of Lake Pleasant and Sacandaga Lake, was built on the ruins of the former Sacandaga Lake Hotel by J. D. Morley. After Morley opened the hotel, it grew from 40 guests to 250 guests. The guest register at Morleys included those from Johnstown, Gloversville, Amsterdam, New Jersey, Maryland, Ohio, the New England states, Pennsylvania, California, and Washington, D.C., as well as those from some of the surrounding Adirondack settlements. Some notable guests' names appear in the register, including Gov. Roswell Flower, state surveyor Verplanck Colvin, Lt. Gov. Timothy Woodruff, author A. A. Chalmers, FJ&G president J. Leslie Hees, and Charles B. Knox of Knox Gelatin. Morleys Hotel published a map when John A. Cole was proprietor to help patrons find their way to the hotel.

DINING ROOM, "MORLEY'S," LAKE PLEASANT, N. Y. ADIRONDACK MOUNTAINS.

Lewey Lake House in the Adirondacks, near Indian Lake, N. Y.

James and Ellen McCormack ran the Lewey Lake House from 1882 to 1895. The McCormacks purchased the land in 1881 from the Ferguson family that was living in guide Alvah Dunning's camp. The McCormacks built an adjoining building of logs containing a parlor and bedrooms and connected it with a walkway. The 40-guest Lewey Lake House was sold to Levi Osgoods in 1902 and again in 1913 for $3,000 to Halsey Galusha and John Burgess. It burned in 1914.

Timberlock on Indian Lake celebrated its 100th anniversary in business in 1999. It started as an adult tent camp and evolved into a "rustic without being rough" hostelry. The enterprise has had only three owners in its history, starting with Erastus "Rat" Farrington. Ted Gavette purchased the business in 1921 and ran it as a family summer camp for 14 years. It was leased to coach Burns Beach for a while and then back to the Gavette family in 1952. The Richard Catlin family took over in 1963 and continues today.

Hotel Sabael, Indian Lake N.Y.

The headline told the story repeated so many times throughout the Adirondacks as, one by one, the hostelries were destroyed by fire. A 1962 newspaper said that "$100,000 Blaze Destroys Hotel in Indian Lake Area." It went on to report that "fire last night destroyed the four story wooden Air-O-Tel Hotel, originally the Hotel Sabael, located about four miles south of Indian Lake on Route 30." The 70-bed building was owned by Robert Bowerman and his wife.

LOCKE HOUSE, INDIAN LAKE, N. Y.

Sometime prior to 1900, James N. Locke and his uncle opened the Locke House. The 25-guest house offered daily mail, rental boats, bathing, good fishing, and hunting with guides, saddle horses, tennis, and other activities. They served farm products with rates from $20 to $25 per week. Henry "Stub" Keenan and his wife, Amy Ordway Keenan, ran it for a while, and Locke again took over the business and ran it until 1930 when he was in his 60s.

Indian Lake is made up of three bodies of water held back by a dam that was originally built by the loggers to transport logs. As the needs grew to provide water recreation for the summer and local residents, the dam was raised. Several hotels were built in the Indian Lake village in the 1880s, and later hotels were established on the lakeshore, following a pattern throughout the Adirondacks as the summer tourism increased.

Indian Lake House, Indian Lake, N. Y.

George Griffin built the 35-guest Indian Lake House on the west shore of Indian Lake in 1890. Edwin R. Wallace, in his 1894 *Guide to the Adirondacks*, suggested climbing the "great and lovely peak styled Squaw Bonnet or Snowy Mountain from the Indian Lake House." James and Ellen Porter McCormack later operated a hotel by the same name until it was sold to Elmer and Maria Osgood. Later it was owned by the Bonesteels before going on to Andrew Christ.

FAULKNER'S INN, BLUE MOUNTAIN LAKE   ADIRONDACK MOUNTAINS, N. Y.

Louise Faulkner was the proprietress of Faulkner's Inn and Cottage in Blue Mountain Lake. Accommodations for 70 were available for $21 per week. Located on the shores of Blue Mountain Lake, surrounded by the mountains, she advertised the hostelry as "the American Switzerland." The inn had its own nine-hole golf course and offered "all sports and entertainment." It opened in 1915, and Faulkner "catered to a refined clientele."

Potter's, the hostelry on the east shore of Blue Mountain Lake, was founded in 1874 by Jno. G. Holland, who was one of the Adirondack pioneer hotel men. When the hotel burned in 1904, Elmer Potter opened an emergency restaurant and converted old guide cabins into guest cabins on the property. By 1920, a larger building was built on the site. They also maintained a large fireproof garage for guests' use. It was sold for private use in 2005.

In 1927, a three-story barn, built in 1865 by the Wheeler Claflin Tannery, became a restaurant. The huge barn had once housed oxen on the ground floor, horses on the second, and hay on the third. Cyrus Durey had traded another building and the surrounding golf course lands for the building and later sold it. It was then converted into the Nick Stoner Inn. In 1993, it was purchased again and the inn was reopened as a large bed-and-breakfast business along with the restaurant.

Merwin Tyler opened a log hotel in 1874 at Blue Mountain Lake. It was expanded in 1876 with a cottage to hold a total of 40 guests. After a fire destroyed part of this building in 1880, he rebuilt a three-story building to accommodate 80 guests. It remained in operation until 1935, when William L. Wessels bought it and carried on the hotel business until 1954. It was purchased for the Adirondack Museum in 1954.

The imposing Prospect House at Blue Mountain Lake, with its two-story privy and electrical service developed by Thomas Edison, met the effects of the United States financial panic of 1893 and the spread of diseases along with the development of railroads that took patrons farther north. Railroads took vacationers to Lake Placid and Saranac Lake, and the Delaware and Hudson Railroad withdrew its daily sleeping car to North Creek. Typhoid fever spread in Blue Mountain Lake and turned people away. Frederick Durant, owner of the house, had to mortgage to his brother for $46,000, and it was not long before Howard Durant took over the hotel. He changed the name to Hotel Utowana to give it a new lease on life. The original manager, G. W. Tunnicliff, was replaced by the room clerk W. T. Graff. By 1897, Howard Durant took over the managing of the hotel. A partnership of J. B. White and the hotel's electrician, the Quinn Brothers, took over before the 1901 season. The typhoid epidemic got worse, and Hotel Utowana closed in 1903 and was torn down in 1915.

The Adirondack Hotel at Long Lake is still welcoming guests much as it has done for over 125 years. Its guest list includes boxer Jack Dempsey, scientist Albert Einstein, and New York governor Alfred E. Smith. It was built in 1879 by Cyrus and Christina Kellogg and named the Lake House. It burned in 1901 and was rebuilt in 1904. Today's owner, Carol Young, remodeled the building in 1990, offering dining rooms with fireplaces, enclosed and outdoor porches, and a rustic taproom. Raquette Lake businessman Patrick Moynehan owned the hotel at one time, and Margaret and Lewis Jennings operated it in the early 1900s. From 1933 to 1946, their son Arthur and his wife owned the historic hotel. Patrons were attracted to the 60-guest hotel by its proximity to Long Lake, a wide spot in the Raquette River.

The Sagamore on Long Lake, N. Y.

The "new" Sagamore at Long Lake, erected in 1889, took the place of the original 1885 hotel. The new 200-guest building was built with more spacious halls, an office, a dining room, and parlors, along with a general smoking and lounging room. The guides and sportsmen made good use of the general room to gather and to make plans for excursions or "to live over again the stirring events of the day." E. Butler, proprietor, had a good reputation for managing a house of "woodsy comfort."

In the Adirondacks. Kellogg's Lake House, Long Lake.

Back in 1860, the Adirondack remote county of Hamilton was the only county in the state not to have legislative representation. Cyrus H. Kellogg of Long Lake became one of the petitioners to appeal for constitutional representation. A primitive hotel was opened in 1857, called Wilber's Raquette Lake House, and sold to Kellogg. He took over the 35-guest hotel in 1867 and enlarged it, eventually constructing a new building on the hillside facing the Long Lake bridge.

The Hotel Altamont at Tupper Lake was open year round in the first half of the 20th century, offering all summer and winter sports. "Stop at the Best" was its slogan where it had the famous Mountain Room with an orchestra and dancing nightly. Hugh A. Beaton Jr., managing owner, also provided "excellent food at popular prices." The four-story hotel with second-floor porches was also recommended by AAA.

Rustic camp architect William Coulter designed the Wawbeek for a New York City businessman, Moritz Walter. Originally a complex of nine buildings, two are left today. The dining room building, pictured here, contains an entwined large stone fireplace chimney and staircase. The big hotel on the property was torn down in 1914 and another built in 1930. It burned after the 1980 Olympics. The owners, Norm and Nancy Howard, sold the Wawbeek in 2007 to a private owner.

Appolos (Paul) Smith formed the Paul Smith Hotel Company from his 1848 "Sporting House," with his wife, Lydia, and three sons, Henry, Phelps, and Appolos Jr., and expanded it to 30,000 acres and 10 lakes. By 1896, it was considered to be the largest hotel in the Adirondacks. His six-horse, tallyho coaches met all the trains at his Adirondack and St. Lawrence Railroad station and took them the three and a half miles to his hotel. Paul Smith's Hotel attracted the rich and famous, including presidents Grover Cleveland, Theodore Roosevelt, and Calvin Coolidge. The wealthy Harrimans, P. T. Barnum of circus fame, the Vanderbilts, and Rockefellers also stayed at the hotel. Appolos died in 1912 at the age of 87, and his son Phelps continued the hotel business until 1937. In his will, Phelps created the Paul Smith's College, the Adirondacks' four-year college. The original buildings on the campus are now being restored.

Two

SOUTHERN AND
CENTRAL ADIRONDACK
TRAIL HOSTELRIES

The Dennies and Dunhams were early hotelkeepers in the southern Hamilton County communities. The two families were related, and after operating the Dunham Cottage with Mrs. S. C. Dennie as proprietor, they moved to Wells in 1835. From there, they moved to Hope where, in the 1840s, Henry Dennie operated the local inn. It became the site of public venues to settle estates and other legal matters.

The 67-room Hamilton Inn was erected in Lake Pleasant in 1917. The Morleys Hotel had burned in 1916, and the owners immediately began to build another to take its place. It was later sold to the Adirondack Club and was renamed the Hamilton Inn. Later owners were Malcolm Atterbury, owner of the Tamarack Playhouse, and William Osborne of another hotel family. In November 1949, when the hotel was closed for the season, Vic Knapp, caretaker, had locked up the chicken coop at 7:30 p.m. At 8:00 p.m. Mr. and Mrs. Leo Rogers discovered the building on fire, and within one hour, only the pillars on the front porch were standing. The loss was $250,000, with only $50,000 in insurance to cover it. The popular inn had a golf course and a boathouse as part of its offerings. Old photographs have differing names for the inn, including Hamilton Inn, the New Morley, and Hamilton County Adirondack Club.

HAMILTON INN BOAT HOUSE ON SACANDAGA LAKE, LAKE PLEASANT, N. Y.

Augustus Avery built Avery's Hotel on the Arietta Road in 1892. By 1915, Lyman, his son, continued the operation, adding a fish hatchery and animal preserve on the property. When it burned down on April 24, 1926, it was rebuilt by Lyman's son Robert. Avery's Hotel was a popular Adirondack hostelry; many were attracted to see and to feed the deer in the surrounding preserve and to fish in the pond. They carried on a hunting and guiding business, and a record black bear was taken by one of the hunting parties. The large dining hall accommodated groups for weddings and other events. The restaurant became known for its fine food, especially its frog legs entrée. It remained in operation up into modern times and accommodated the thousands of snowmobilers who were attracted to the Adirondack snowmobile trails. It is now closed.

DINING ROOM - AVERY MOTEL - ARIETTA, N. Y. - RT. 10

James Aird traveled from Scotland in the middle of the 19th century to settle in the Adirondacks. He acquired 1,000 acres of land and, by 1890, his son David had built a large resort, Airdwood, on Lily Lake, now Airdwood Lake. Airdwood remained open as a hotel until recently, when it became a religious retreat.

For over 100 years, the Irondequoit Club has been welcoming guests to the Adirondacks. Founded in 1892 by a group of sportsmen from New York City and New Jersey, it has remained in the hands of the members of the Piseco Company and is open today as an inn for summer visitors. The building was constructed in 1903 on a portion of the 1850s residence of Gene Abrams. Cabins were added on the 11,000-acre property, and visitors can rent rooms, cabins, or tent sites.

The imposing three-story hotel in Piseco was operated as the Anibal House from 1925 to 1946. It had been built by a Curtis family in 1871 as a family home. Truman Lawrence built an addition in 1910, and it became a well-known hunting and fishing lodge under the ownership of Len Anibal. George and Helen Haskell kept the hotel with 20 bedrooms and a dining room going from 1946 to 1978, when it too met its fate with fire.

Floyd W. and Mary Gilman Abrams built the Sportsmen's Home at Piseco in 1880. The hostelry was also known as the Abrams House. Room, board, and guide service was offered to the sports who came from the city to hunt and fish the Adirondacks. At the same time, the owners were raising their 10 children in the home. Later it became a private home before it succumbed to fire in 1956.

Lake Pleasant Inn, Built 1840,
Lake Pleasant, N. Y. Adirondack Mountains.

Hamilton County sheriff Ephraim Phillips opened the Lake Pleasant House in 1843. The Piseco Lake Trout Club, one of America's first sporting clubs, ate there in 1843 and in 1846 called it "Pearls." By 1848, Phillips had moved to Piseco to open another hotel, the Piseco Lake Inn. The stately Lake Pleasant House featured the tall porch pillars and surrounding verandas, common to many of the early hotels. The lobby followed the traditional Adirondack rustic style with log wainscoting and logs around the fireplace. A mounted deer head with antlers above the fireplace mantle became somewhat of a trademark on many of the woodland hostelries. Phillips went on in 1890 at the age of 88 to write a small novel, A Tale of Love at Piseco, in which he described the hotel and its picturesque setting at Piseco.

OFFICE AND LOBBY, LAKE PLEASANT INN, LAKE PLEASANT,
N. Y. ADIRONDACK MOUNTAINS.

Phillips's hotel was later taken over by William Courtney. By 1876, he was managing the hotel and did so until 1890. Later managers of the hotel were William Lamkey, Tim Crowley, Garfield and Robert Kenell, and Len Anibal. It met the fate of other hotels in a bad fire in the 1920s. There were two William Courtneys, William P. and William N. William P. was 17 years older than William N., possibly his father. They both ran hotels with William N. the proprietor of the Adirondack House on Lake Piseco in the early 1900s. Courtney's hotel was a large two-story building in Piseco. It was a family hotel "among the wilds of Piseco and Lake Pleasant." William P. was born in Lake Pleasant in 1836 and moved to Arietta in 1865 with his wife, Julie A. Gallup, where he went into the hotel business. Both of the Courtney men served as town clerk, and William N. did some outdoor guiding.

Mountain Home was an unusual Adirondack hostelry that began as a private home. Orasmus Benajah Matteson, an attorney from Utica, built a mountain retreat on Wilmurt Lake in Morehouse. In 1885, the place was incorporated as Mountain Home with a group of six friends serving as directors. In 1888, it was incorporated again under the name Matteson's Adirondack Hotel. The building was destroyed by fire in 1923.

The unidentified hotel in the southern Adirondacks shown here may have been at Morehouse. A full-fledged hotel had been opened there in 1869 with French-born Eugene Maheux as proprietor. In 1873, a nighttime fire destroyed the establishment, and a new hotel was built. Henry F. Kreuzer took over in 1890. One traveler recalled that "Mr. Kreuzer was a lumberman and the hotel was full of lumberjacks."

According to the Delaware and Hudson Rairoad's 1929 booklet, *A Summer Paradise*, the "new picturesque Huletts" on Lake George was "right in the Warpath of History," only a few miles from Fort Ticonderoga. Running water was in every room with private baths and electric lights. A. H. Wyatt, proprietor, "guaranteed you more at Huletts for your money than any place in the Adirondacks." Huletts was on the lake, near the islands, and had the best fishing grounds. It provided motor launches, canvas-covered canoes, and boats.

The Trojan, one of Lake George's many hotels, was located at Cleverdale on the back side of the lake on a long peninsula. The Trojan had electric service, flush toilets, and running water upstairs and down, an important offering for the early hotels in the Adirondacks. Owner Harold L. Stickney added larger porches, offered "non-leaking" boats and canoes, and prepared three substantial meals per day served by experienced waitresses who were carrying on the reputation the Trojan had built over 18 years of serving guests.

53

The original six-story Fort William Henry Hotel, once on the site of today's Fort William Henry Hotel at Lake George, contained 350 rooms. It was massive and impressive with a 24-foot-wide portico, including a line of 30-foot-high Corinthian columns. The chef came from the famous Ponce de Leon Hotel at St. Augustine, and the manager of the same hotel, O. D. Seavey, managed the Fort William Henry. He was a host "known the world over." An orchestra played every afternoon and evening, and the hotel had its own dock on Lake George. A great drawing room with writing desks, parlors, a fine billiard hall, a 1,000-seat dining hall, tennis and croquet lawns, bowling alleys, shooting galleries, and facilities for all such sports combined to make it a major Adirondack hostelry. It was known as the "most exquisite gem of all American resorts." The great hotel burned in 1911 and was rebuilt in a smaller version.

The 2,600-foot summit of Prospect Mountain overlooking Lake George became the site of a hotel in 1877 with a carriage road leading to the top. By 1895, a cable inclined railway was built up the east face of the mountain and thousands took advantage of this major Adirondack attraction at 50¢ per ride. It was advertised as "the finest mountain view in America." Along with the hotel, a restaurant and dance hall were added. The railway failed financially and went out of business in 1903. Dr. James Ferguson had purchased the top of the mountain in the 1870s. His first hotel was destroyed in a forest fire in 1880, and he rebuilt in order to run a health center that remained until 1895. The 160-acre business was purchased by George Foster Peabody, and he, being opposed to the gambling going on there, turned the property over to New York State in the 1920s. The over-five-mile toll highway has been designated the Prospect Mountain Veterans Memorial Highway.

The Sagamore on Lake George, Sagamore, N. Y.

The Sagamore at Green Island in Lake George at Bolton Landing has been a distinguished Adirondack resort hotel since 1883. Accommodating 400 in the early years and 900 today, the hotel offered a golf course, a dance orchestra, and a planned social program with a social director on staff. The complex was built on Green Island at a time when it was a tree-covered wilderness. In 1930, it was remodeled and served conventions until the 1950s. The Sagamore, once owned by five millionaires, was under the proprietorship of Myron O. Brown, whose reputation as a hotel manager was far reaching. Since 1981, with restoration and the addition of accommodations, it has operated as a high-end resort. Today's Sagamore on Green Island is the third on the site. The original buildings burned in 1914, and the present main building was constructed in 1922 and enlarged in 1930.

LAKE GEORGE
SAGAMORE
Bolton Landing, New York

Scene of the 1951 Ætna Life
Regional meeting. Attendance
restricted to Regionnaires—
Ætna's outstanding salesmen.

Hotel Marion, Lake George, N. Y.

Hotel Marion, on a 125-acre site, was six miles from Lake George Village on "one of the best stone roads in the state." The steamers on Lake George also took patrons eight miles by water to the Hotel Marion dock on the west shore of the lake. The bedchambers in the 400-guest hotel were "large, bright, cheerful, and airy, with or without private baths." Many of the guests who traveled to the Marion House came from Brooklyn to enjoy the "mirth, music and dancing!"

Trout House,
Hague on Lake George, N.Y.

Attracting the summer crowd to the Adirondack hostelries required some creative advertising. Richard J. Bolton, proprietor of the Trout House Cottages and Casino at Hague on Lake George, had a flair for persuasive advertising. He wrote, "Its gentle sloping bathing beach is almost irresistible to the bather. Immediately back of the house one breaks into almost a virgin forest that covers the foothills leading upward to the lofty peaks whose summits command some of the most entrancing views of the world."

"PHOENIX HOTEL", LOOKING NORTH FROM P. O. HAGUE, N. Y.

Hotel Phoenix at Hague on Lake George was managed by Mrs. George D. Streeter. It was a two-minute walk from the steamer landing, and a representative from the hotel met each boat. Accommodating 50, the hotel had it all, including sanitary plumbing, tennis, baseball, boating, fishing, bathing, motoring, hiking, horseback riding, a post office, daily mail, telegraph-telephone, and Catholic and Protestant churches. It was one of the earliest of the Lake George hotels.

Wiawaka Holiday House is a unique Adirondack hostelry. Situated at the head of beautiful Lake George on a 59-acre site, it is an ideal place to spend a vacation. The name, meaning "the eternal spirit of women," reveals its mission. Opened in 1903, it was a place for women to vacation. Working girls and self-supporting widows were encouraged to come during July and August for two-week stays, while professional women came in June and September.

Edwin J. Worden operated the Worden Hotel and the Arlington Hotel at Lake George in the first decade of the 1900s. The three-story Worden Hotel accommodated 200 at $14–$18 per week, and the Arlington Hotel charged $10–$12 per week. The Worden Hotel was only a quarter mile from the train station, making it a popular stop for travelers. Lake George, possibly the most visited place in the Adirondacks, dates back to the Native Americans and a visit by French missionaries in 1646.

The Hillside House was on high ground at Hague on Lake George. Thomas Bolton, proprietor, maintained an excellent table. The hotel farm supplied fresh eggs, milk, and vegetables, and the pure springwater came from an elevation of 135 feet. The 80-guest hotel had a quiet, shady lawn and an in-house orchestra. It also rented garage space, automobiles, and boat launches. Free transportation by bus from the steamboat landing was available. John McLenathan became a later proprietor.

Roger's Rock, Mountain, and Hotel, Lake George, N.Y.

The Rogers Rock property on Lake George was "bought by a New York gentleman" who had long known the place. He leased the property to the Rogers Rock Hotel Company, which hired a manager. The hotel was on a rise, 80 feet above the lake. It had its own garden and employed a French chef. The casino on the lakeshore offered billiard tables and bowling alleys. One of the features of the property was a series of woodland trails.

In 1913, the "new" Adirondack Hotel was accommodating guests at the foot of Mount Hackensack in Warrensburg. It was three miles from the Thurman railroad station. The three-story hotel was up-to-date with steam heat, hot and cold water, electric lights, and bells in every room. The hotel was under the management of the O'Conner brothers. Note the garage on the side, a desired benefit for the guests' automobiles when they came into widespread use.

Bonnie Brae Villa in Warrensburg was under the proprietorship of a woman director, Mrs. H. F. Parker. It was a fine old village farmhouse on Main Street with four fireplaces, three baths, and electric light. In five minutes, guests could walk to the post office, trolley, lake, library, and church. It offered its own farm and dairy products with home cooking. When automobiles came into use, garage space as offered.

M. O'Conner was the proprietor of the year-round "new" Warren House at Warrensburg in 1913. The four-story house accommodated 75 guests for $8 to $12 per week. Transients were welcomed for $2 per night.

Grand View Inn,   Chestertown, N. Y.

Auto stages brought tourists from the Riverside railroad station some seven miles to the Grand View Inn. Located on the main highway at Chestertown, the Grand View Inn offered pure water and home cooking, two advantages sought by the city dwellers when they came to the Adirondacks. David Shugrue, proprietor, maintained accommodations for 100 guests. Included with the main building were some 10 guest cottages.

The 50-guest Panther Mountain Hotel on the main highway at Chestertown was newly furnished with all modern improvements in 1927. It advertised that it was "on the main route from New York City to Montreal." Buses met the trains at the Riverside railroad station to take guests to and from the hotel. The hotel featured water from its own springs and both American and European plans. Some rooms had private baths and, unlike the seasonal hotels, they were open year-round.

The imposing 150-guest Chester House, once the largest structure in Chestertown, burned down in the middle of the last century. Built in the 1830s, it catered to the city folk through the heyday of the Adirondacks. C. Albert Jacob penned his memories of his 1890s trips as a boy to the "homelike" Chester House. His family summered in Chestertown from the 1880s until 1905, when they purchased a permanent summer camp on nearby Loon Lake. The Chester Inn, on the same hotel site today, was built in 1837 for Charles Fowler, an Albany merchant. Harry Downs purchased the Fowler estate in the 1880s, a deal that included the Chester House. Behind today's Chester Inn, the original barns from the early hotel are still standing. Bruce and Suzanne Robbins have restored the original Fowler house on Chestertown's Main Street into a bed-and-breakfast.

J. O'Connell's Rising House accommodated 50 guests, just five minutes from the Riverside train station, a station that served a number of the surrounding hostelries and contributed to their success. C. J. O'Connell was listed as the owner in the 1940s and offered steam heat, excellent meals, a cocktail bar, and comfortable rooms. About the same time, Walter Grube became the owner and offered meals at all hours.

NORTHWOODS INN
ATHOL, N. Y.

Square dancing became a big attraction at the Adirondack lodges and inns following World Wars I and II. The Northwoods Inn at Athol became famous for square dances. The log building, with its rustic interior and large dancing area, fit well in the Adirondack setting. The inn was built in 1948 by Hilda and Jake Drexel, German immigrants. After being closed for some 20 years, the Northwoods Inn was reopened in 1994 by Howard and Julie Gallup Cook.

The old Wells House, still standing at Pottersville, dates back to 1845. In a 1921 Adirondack guidebook, it was listed as being run by Allen T. Wells. It had fish and game dinners in season and was on the "trunk line from New York City to Montreal." Extreme restoration was completed on the deteriorating hostelry in 2005, and it is now open under the proprietorship of Shirley and Paul Bubar. The original guest registers add to the history of the over-160-year-old Adirondack hotel.

Benjamin Straight, proprietor, met his guests with an automobile at North Creek to take them to the Thirteenth Lake House at North River. The lodge accommodated 40 guests at $18 per week. It, like many of the Adirondack hostelries, was able to offer running springwater and an excellent table. A guest writing a postcard agreed, with "just waiting for the dinner bell."

Pueblo Hotel, Brant Lake, N. Y.

The 159-room Pueblo Hotel was midway on Brant Lake near the islands, the best fishing grounds on the lake. The hotel provided a boat and automobile livery and rented gas launches. Philetus Smith, the proprietor, promised two mails daily, telephone, and telegraph. Fully furnished summer cottages were also available. Note the boathouse on the shore of the lake; boathouses were offered at many of the lakefront hostelries where guests could drive boats directly inside.

The Barque of Pine Knot on the Cortland College property at Pine Knot on Raquette Lake needs mention as one of the most unusual of the Adirondack hostelries. It is a houseboat built in the 1870s by Adirondack Great Camps builder, William West Durant. The houseboat, with sleeping quarters, bath, and kitchen, was parked in Raquette Lake during the black fly season for the occupants of the camp and their guests. The boat is on dry land today and serves as a small museum.

66

In 1905, there were six hotels in the town of Inlet. Frank A. Williams, at 29 years old, ran the Seventh Lake House. Convicted murderer and model for the similar character in *An American Tragedy*, Chester Gillette dined at the Seventh Lake House the day before he was arrested for the murder of Grace Brown. The Seventh Lake House employed a French chef, Dominick Fredette. In 1925, Frank Breen became proprietor of the house. By mid-century, J. Perry Smith ran the establishment.

EAGLE BAY HOTEL FROM EAGLE MOUNTAIN, LOOKING TOWARDS GRAND VIEW AND NEODACK, ADIRONDACKS, N.Y.

One of the largest hotels on the Fulton Chain of Lakes was pleasantly located at Eagle Bay on Fourth Lake and was appropriately called the Eagle Bay Hotel. The 175-guest hostelry opened each year on May 15 and remained open until October 1. Rates ranged from $4 to $5 per day and $17–$30 per week. Built in 1896, the Eagle Bay Hotel was one of several large hotels on the popular Fulton Chain.

The Cliff House Terrace at Eagle Bay was a quiet place to spend a vacation in the 1940s. Located on the Fulton Chain, it offered a wide range of Adirondack activities with nearby Inlet and Old Forge. The Cliff House Terrace enjoyed many years of a successful business before following a pattern often repeated in the Adirondacks; the property was broken up into several parcels and sold off to private owners.

Manhassit was located at the foot of Fourth Lake on the Fulton Chain, commanding a magnificent view of the lake and surrounding mountains. Its season ran from the usual May to October. All modern conveniences could be found at the 100-guest hotel for $15 per week and up. The good fishing and the pleasant surroundings caused the growth of many hostelries on Fourth Lake.

The 40-guest Minnowbrook Camp on Fourth Lake was open June through October at $13 per week. The house offered open fireplaces, sanitary plumbing, and "everything for the comfort and convenience of the guests." The proprietor was David Griffiths. Minnowbrook was a name used elsewhere in the Adirondacks on other places, a common occurrence when communications did not cross the mountains from one place to another.

The three-story gabled Rocky Point Inn on Fourth Lake at Inlet offered electric lights, hot and cold water, comfortable furnishings, and sanitary plumbing, all accommodation attributes taken for granted today. "Fine state road and adequate railroad facilities" were also promoted; visitors left New York City after breakfast and ate supper at the Rocky Point Inn. With its view, rustic rocking chairs lining the porches, two beaches, surrounding woods, and social events, the Rocky Point Inn offered "many superior attractions."

The Wood, Fourth Lake, Adirondack Mountains

406653

Hotelkeeper Fred Hess built his Adirondack camp, the Hess Camp, on Fourth Lake in 1894. Four years later, Philo Wood took it over and called it the Wood Hotel. Over the years it was expanded, which can easily be seen by comparing photographs that appeared in print in the publications of that day. The Wood Hotel took on a new owner, William Dunay, in 1946, and it was in full operation until 1980. When Dunay passed away in 1989, the contents were auctioned off and the property sat empty. His family wisely held on to the property until a buyer could be found who would maintain the property as an Adirondack hotel. In 2003, the right buyers were found when Joedda McClain and Jay Latterman purchased the hotel with plans to restore the historic hotel. It became a major undertaking, enlisting some 25 local, skilled workers, working six days a week, sometimes without heat, for 11 months to do the major renovation it required. The fully restored and updated "Adirondack Showplace," the Woods Inn, opened for business again in June 2005.

THE ARROWHEAD--4TH LAKE, ADIRONDACKS.

The "American Tragedy" brought the Arrowhead Hotel in Inlet to national fame. Pregnant working girl Grace Brown was murdered by her wealthy boyfriend, Chester Gillette, and later evidence showed that he had spent time at the hotel. The tragic story became the subject of Theodore Dreiser's best-selling novel, *An American Tragedy*. In its heyday, the Arrowhead Hotel boasted a four-piece orchestra and a gold and white dining room. The parlor, typical of the big Adirondack hotels, had a piano, writing desks, comfortable chairs, and an Adirondack decor. The Arrowhead Hotel at the head of Fourth Lake accommodated 175 guests. Rates for one in a room were $15–$20 per week. It was open June 1 to October 1 with special rates before July 15 and after September 15. Today the site is a town park and beach.

"Arrowhead Parlor". Fourth Lake, Adirondacks.

No. 1171   Moore & Gibson Co., New York.   Germany

The well-situated Aquapine Hotel, one of the many hotels on Fourth Lake, has a story to tell. Unfortunately, it serves as an example of the many small Adirondack hotels whose stories have been lost to the passing of years. The four-story building with two American flags, one on the roof and the other on a tall flagpole, indicate a well-run hostelry. The veranda running around the house would welcome guests to sit and relax overlooking the lake. The photographs were published by the Standard Photo Supply Company of Otter Lake, New York. The rustic bridge in the photograph crossed a bay near the hotel, and the covered dock building, built in the Adirondack rustic style, served the guide boats used by the guests.

Bald Mountain House, Third Lake, Fulton Chain, Adirondacks.

Barrett's Bald Mountain House, on Third Lake in the Fulton Chain, was one of the oldest and most prominent hotels in the Adirondacks at the beginning of the 20th century. The 150-guest hotel was seasonal, open from June to October. It offered rooms at $15 per week and up with C. M. Barrett as the proprietor. Note the long boardwalk to the dock providing convenient access to the waterfront for the guests.

51128   The Glenmore, Big Moose Lake, Adirondack Mts., N. Y.

The Glenmore once stood as the most notable upscale hotel on Big Moose Lake. The five-story building with clapboard sides was built in 1899 by D. B. Sperry. The Glenmore served as a central location for many of the lake's activities. The boathouse had a casino and dance hall on the second floor where guests enjoyed square dancing. Chester Gillette of *An American Tragedy* fame rented a boat there before the murder. It burned down in 1950.

Lake View Lodge with seven cottages was located on a rocky point jutting into Big Moose Lake. On a 40-foot hill, the Lake View Lodge commanded a clear view of the lake. Enjoying attributes claimed by many of the big Adirondack hostelries, the Lake View Lodge had its own springs for fresh springwater and had its own garden and dairy for fresh produce. Charles Williams served as proprietor during the hotel era.

George and Louisa Yocum, the owner-managers of the Moose Head Hotel in Old Forge, mailed out letters each year to attract business. Open all year, they could offer a large lobby with a wood-burning fireplace and a dining hall that "satisfied the lusty appetites of the outdoor sportsmen." The Rathskeller featured knotty pine panels, red-checkered tablecloths, candles in bottles, and a jukebox. It catered to skiing and skating groups, and its beds were supplied with plenty of blankets and innerspring mattresses.

The Old Forge House is situated on the entrance to the Fulton Chain of Lakes, named after Robert Fulton, who once promoted a canal through the Adirondack lakes. The 150-guest hotel was open year-round at $15 per week. It was an up-to-date hostelry with steam heat and electric lights. Patrons reached the hotel via the Mohawk and Malone Division of the New York Central Railroad. A special Fulton Chain Railroad took passengers on the last section to reach Old Forge.

The stately Van Auken's Inne, with its pillars and two-floor porches, was built in 1891 next to the railroad tracks at Thendara. In 1905, the three-story inn was moved 75 feet away and is now across the road from the Thendara railroad station. Van Auken's Inne was completely renovated in 1988 by the Taylors, the owners at the time, back to its original splendor of the Victorian age. Today it is run by the Marks family for food and lodging.

Steamboats began operating on Lake George in 1817, transporting the traveling public to the Adirondack hostelries. The first boat, *James Caldwell*, an 80-foot craft built by the Lake George Steamboat Company, burned in 1821. The *Mountaineer* followed in 1824 and ran until 1837. The *William Caldwell* steamboat ran from 1838 to 1848. Other boats followed in the 1850s and through the 1890s and early 1900s, including the *Minne-Ha-Ha, Ganouski, Owl, Horicon I, Horicon II, Ticonderoga, Mohican I, Mohican II, Mohican III, Sagamore,* and in later years, *Lac du St. Sacrement.* Today the *Ticonderoga, Minne-Ha-Ha,* and *Mohican II* continue the boating tradition of Lake George. The photograph below shows the burning of the first *Ticonderoga* in August 1901; *Ticonderoga II* was placed in service in 1950.

RUINS OF STR. TICONDEROGA, BURNED AUG. 29th 1901, LAKE GEORGE. N.Y.

Three

OLYMPIC AND HIGH PEAKS HOSTELRIES

Shown here, the corner of the dining room of the Wilmington Inn illustrates the "white tablecloth" elegance of the major Adirondack hotels and inns. Located directly at the entrance to the Whiteface Mountain Memorial Highway and the Whiteface Ski Center, the Wilmington Inn attracted summer and winter patrons. P. E. Weaver was an early owner, and William H. DeSilvo owned it in the 1940s. T. F. Roland was the proprietor in the 1920s.

The 60-guest Homestead was 10 miles from the Ausable Forks Station. It was located at Wilmington. It had two "easy riding" buses going each way daily. The noted Adirondack peak Whiteface was a short distance away. Mountain climbing became part of the hotel's offerings, and guides were available. After 1935, motoring up the new highway to the top of Whiteface Mountain, which filled one with awe, attracted guests to the Homestead.

Whiteface Mountain House in the Adirondacks, Wilmington, New York—78

The popular Whiteface Mountain House was situated on a hill overlooking the Ausable River Valley at Wilmington. The rooms for 75 guests commanded beautiful views of the grand ranges and mighty peaks of the Adirondack Mountains. Hammocks and swings were supplied for the guests along with a sand garden for children. The Whiteface Mountain House was open all year with a post office and telegraph in-house. F. E. Everest was one of the early proprietors.

78

Martin's Hotel, on the Lower Saranac Lake, simply called Martin's, was one of the earliest hostelries in the Adirondacks. William F. Martin came to the gateway of the Saranac and Tupper Lakes region of the Adirondacks in 1849 to build a small house to accommodate sportsmen. He was a good woodsman and hunter and developed a successful business, which grew to accommodate 200 guests. It later became the Saranac Lake House.

The Hotel Ampersand on the Lower Saranac Lake was "furnished with the most comfortable modern conveniences" and offered fresh Jersey (cow) milk and vegetables from the hotel farm. It catered to the young people with tennis, baseball, shooting, swimming, sailing, rowing, music, and so on. There was a general store in the hotel where outfits and supplies were furnished for camping. The hotel was "especially attractive during the fall time of the year." C. M. Eaton was manager in 1896.

The Saranac Inn Company owned a 15-square-mile lot on Upper Saranac Lake. The inn stood on a point extending out into the lake and, according to Seneca Ray Stoddard's 1892 guidebook, *The Adirondacks*, "commanded a broad expanse of water and distant mountains equaled nowhere in the Adirondacks except from the highland between Mirror Lake and Lake Placid." In the 1890s, the inn accommodated 125 guests, and it expanded over the years to over six times

NAL MEETING - U.S.F + G. - F F G.
7-8-9 - 1948

its original size. It became an ideal location for large gatherings and conventions. One such convention held in 1948 is shown here with over 100 attendees. After 1892, it was reached by the Mohawk and Malone Division of the New York Central Railroad. The trains could connect to the steamers *Saranac* and *Loon* on the Upper Saranac Lake. The inn closed in 1960 and burned down in 1978.

Adirondack Mountains, The Algonquin on Lower Saranac Lake

Those who searched for excellent small-mouthed black bass fishing found the Algonquin on the Saranac Chain of Lakes. The "island-studded waters were especially suited for light boating, canoeing, motor-boating, and houseboat life and for good fishing." Much like many of the Adirondack fine hotels, the Algonquin was known for its table. A 1902 menu, for example, featured consommé paysanne, sirloin of beef pique a la flamande, and charlotte russe.

47. RIVERSIDE INN, SARANAC LAKE, ADIRONDACK MOUNTAINS, N. Y.

Riverside Inn at Saranac Lake was one of the leading hotels in town. It had a fine location and steam heat. Accommodating 125 people, 50 of the 75 rooms had private baths. An elevator served the four floors of the big hotel. The inn was operated by Pine and Corbett, Inc., and was promoted in the 1924 A Summer Paradise by the Delaware and Hudson Railroad as a "modern structure, large, attractive, and handsomely equipped at the beginning of the 20th Century." A bus from the inn met all trains.

82

"A Forward Movement to Meet Saranac Lake's Greatest Need"

$125,000 IN 10 DAYS

November 13-23, 1925, Inclusive

THE HOTEL BUILDERS, Limited

A stock-selling organization composed of local citizens formed to secure $125,000 in subscriptions to the 7 per cent preferred stock in Saranac Lake's new hotel

In November 1925, Saranac Lake residents raised $125,000 in 10 days to meet Saranac Lake's greatest need, the building of a new hotel. They had lost nine earlier hotels to fire or demolition. Local citizens formed a stock-selling organization to meet the need of a fine hotel in town; the mottos "a hotel is the shop window of the town" and "towns are known by the hotels they keep" guided their decisions. The hotel was built to last, with no wood used in the construction except for wainscoting in order to avoid another hotel lost to fire. It was also built strong enough to hold two more floors if needed in the future. It was expected to cost a total of $425,000 to build, and even though there had been seven unsuccessful attempts to raise funds for a hotel, the directors believed that their seven percent guaranteed dividend would help this project to succeed—and it did. Another guarantee was that the investors would get paid before the builders got their profit.

Main Street looking N.
Saranac Lake, N.Y.

The Berkeley Hotel was built in the 1870s and opened year-round on Saranac Lake's Main Street. It was built and operated by Charles Gray for a year. It was eventually purchased by a Mr. Streeter in 1882. Streeter added a large wing on the north side. His partner, a Mr. Dennison, then took over only to be followed shortly thereafter by his widow. When she remarried and left, Walter Sagendorf purchased the popular hostelry in 1913. C. E. Welch was the proprietor in the early 1920s, until the hotel was ravaged by a deadly fire in 1925. The Berkeley Hotel had a restaurant in connection with the hostelry where table d'hote meals (complete dinners) were served as well as à la carte service. In June 1891, the Adirondack guides met at the Berkeley Hotel and formed the Adirondack Guides Association. Verplanck Colvin, superintendent of the New York State Survey, a friend and honorary member of the guides, was the main speaker, attended by guides and other dignitaries of that day.

84

HOTEL CHILDWOLD, Adirondack Mountains, Childwold, N. Y.

Addison Child purchased 16,000 acres of Adirondack land in St. Lawrence County in the 1800s and became one of those entrepreneurs who saw the opportunities the Adirondacks offered. He sold some of the land for $1 to $3 per acre to bring in settlers. He added a sawmill to produce lumber to sell to his tenants. And in 1889, he built the great, 300-guest Hotel Childwold, which used the products from his farms. When Child passed away, his friend who had worked with him, Henry G. Dorr, became the new owner. Charlie Leland and William F. Ingold, well-known hotel managers, were hired to manage the hotel. The hotel had piazzas (porches) on three sides and a belvedere (a building with a view) rising 78 feet above the lake.

The Owl's Head at Keene was on the international highway between New York and Montreal. It was also on the motorbus route from Westport and Lake Placid and could accommodate 70 travelers. W. B. Washburn, proprietor, offered both European (rate covers room and service but not meals) and American (rate covers room, service, and meals) plans. It advertised "numerous points of interest in the vicinity."

M. F. Luck, proprietor of the Interbrook Lodge and Cottages in Keene Valley, offered "a delightful place to spend the summer." It was "the best moderate price hotel in the mountains." The Interbrook Lodge and Cottages was surrounded by the high peaks in the heart of the Adirondacks. The property contained an old-fashioned, open camp log house—an Adirondack lean-to.

St. Hubert's Inn is located on Keene Heights, at the head of Keene Valley, surrounded by the high peaks of the Mount Marcy Range. Syracuse College of Forestry student Joseph Bernier reported that it employed "reliable guides for camping, hunting, fishing and tramping [a walk in the woods]." He also told of guiding blind and deaf Helen Keller at St. Hubert's Inn in 1924 on her visit to the Adirondacks. The Ausable Club now owns the inn and has preserved it.

The 50-guest Cascade House was built in 1878 on a small piece of land between Upper and Lower Cascade Lakes by Nicaner and Ellen Miller. It was enlarged three times its size for the 1888 season. Wallace's guidebook reported "unexceptionable" table service and that the "waitresses are neat and rosy-cheeked country maidens." It went through several owners, including the Lake Placid Club, and was finally demolished in 1947 when it became part of the New York State Forest Preserve.

Adirondack Mountains, Stevens House Lake Placid

F. Paul Stevens was president of the Stevens Hotel Company at Lake Placid. His large hotel accommodated 450, the largest hotel in Lake Placid. The rooms were $56 and up per week in the 1920s. Transients could stay for $9 per day, and there were special rates for families. Baths were in 70 of the suites. Each room offered long-distance telephone. The Stevens House and Annex stood between Lake Placid and Mirror Lake. They advertised their "beautiful drives."

HOTEL BELMONT, LAKE PLACID, N. Y. IN THE ADIRONDACKS 59

Patrons had entire relief from hay fever at the Belmont Hotel in Lake Placid. They could also enjoy the view of Lake Placid, Whiteface, and other surrounding mountains from the veranda. It was a three-minute walk to either lake, Placid or Mirror. John Schatz, proprietor, promoted "table unexcelled" and "large airy rooms." The hotel featured tennis courts in the pine grove behind the hotel building.

The Whiteface Inn at Lake Placid, originally built in 1882, was replaced in 1901 with a more elegant hotel. It burned in 1909 and was replaced with a 350-guest hotel. It was razed in 1985. The Whiteface Inn accommodated 300 guests at $42 per week. All suites came with a bath and were open from June to October. Manager J. J. Sweeney worked in a South Carolina hotel during the December-to-May season, another option for the Adirondack hotelkeepers.

THE HOMESTEAD, LAKE PLACID, N. Y.

The Homestead at Lake Placid, under the proprietorship of H. J. Green, accommodated 40. It had a special for families during June and September. In the 1940s, it was owned by M. A. Roland. The Homestead, once one of the most beautiful spots on Lake Placid's Main Street with its lawns and verandas, was torn down to make room for the Hilton Hotel before the 1980 Olympics. It was recommended by Duncan Hines for good food and friendly atmosphere.

6758. MIRROR LAKE AND GRAND VIEW HOTEL, ADIRONDACK MOUNTAINS.

COPYRIGHT, 1902, BY DETROIT PHOTOGRAPHIC CO.

Jeanette C. Will

The Grand View Hotel at Lake Placid accommodated 350 people and was advertised in 1896 as the "most modern and comfortable resort in the Adirondacks." At that time, it became fully lighted with electricity in every room and complete elevator service. Public hot and cold baths were available on each floor, and some suites had private baths. Persons afflicted with "pulmonary troubles" (tuberculosis) had never been entertained, and patrons had perfect relief from hay fever. A new billiard and pool room was added, and a large dance hall with a full orchestra was offered. The hotel was operated by the Placid Hotel Corporation with Allen, Todd and Irons of Lake Placid and New York City as the proprietors. The hotel was in a 100-acre private park, and it was the only hotel of its size in the Adirondacks to be fully protected against fire by automatic sprinklers.

GRAND VIEW HOTEL, LAKE PLACID, N. Y.

The Lakeside Inn, with accommodations for 60, promoted Lake Placid as "the Garden Spot of the Adirondacks, (a title incontestable) possessing as it does the finest combination of lake and mountain scenery in a region famous for its beautiful views." With its reputation for being one of the best-conducted houses in Lake Placid, it was able to stay open all year round. Special prices prevailed during the off-seasons.

By 1900, Lake Placid had become a major summer resort. In 1899, Albert Stickney from Michigan and his wife, Etta, built an inn called the Pines in a pine grove near the lake. In 1920, Robert B. Scott owned it, and Paul Augsberger bought the inn in 1923 and renamed it the St. Moritz Hotel. A six-story addition was put on in 1926, and an annex was added. Nude sunbathing was offered on the roof in 1931. In 2004, after several owners, it was purchased by Frank Segger and Jill Cardinale Segger and renamed the Pines of Lake Placid.

HIDDEN PINES — Jubin's, 5 Highland Place — Lake Placid, N. Y. — Phone 755

The Hidden Pines on Highland Place at Lake Placid added to the hostelries that opened to accommodate the influx of year-round vacationers to the popular resort. Owned by the Jubin family, the lodge was ideally located for both summer and winter sports. It became famous for its good food, a major drawing card for Adirondack boardinghouses. In the early 1920s promotional literature, Lake Placid was called "Nature's Masterpiece."

Hillcrest Lodge at Lake Placid was one of many hostelries that opened for business in the fast-growing Lake Placid winter resort area. Located on Grand View Hill, the lodge operated year-round by Verda Zinale was within five minutes of the arena, the toboggan slide, the skating rink, the ski trails, the ski jump, the post office, and the theater. The lodge wisely offered free equipment for participation in winter sports and free instructions for the novice.

Adirondack Mountains, Lake Placid Inn

The Lake Placid Inn with Frank W. Swift as proprietor and manager was a stone's throw from the water. Suites of one to three rooms were available. They emphasized that "pulmonary cases positively not taken" to avoid the contagious disease. The Lake Placid Inn, also known as the Lake Placid House, was located between Mirror Lake and Lake Placid and was first owned by the Brewster family, one of the earliest settlers at Lake Placid. It was destroyed by fire sometime before the 1940s.

The Lake Placid-Marcy Hotel slogan was "For the Rest of Your Life" and enticed city dwellers to Lake Placid "midst breathtaking scenery in nature's most stimulating sport center." The six-story brick hotel was one of Lake Placid's most luxurious and fireproof hotels, where every room had an outside view and a private bath. J. A. Gilman managed the 300-guest hotel in the 1930s, and it was open all year.

Dewey decimal library system developer, Melvil Dewey, and his wife founded the Lake Placid Club in 1890. It was a membership hostelry eventually with some 2,000 members. Noted for winter sports, it pioneered their development and attracted the 1932 Winter Olympics. In 1987, the Lake Placid Club was purchased by a development company with a plan to reopen it as a first-class resort by 1989. It had gone through a bankruptcy, and unfortunately, in November 1992, after a series of arson fires, the vacant main building burned beyond repair.

Lake Placid Club River farms   Intervales from north bank of West Ausable

Adirondack country was farming country during the hotel era when the big camp complexes and hotels found it profitable to grow their own produce and raise their own animals. The Lake Placid Club served great food to their guests, thanks to their farmland shown here. Fresh dairy products were found on the tables throughout the mountains, and prize sheep and goats, along with exotic fowl, were raised. Many of the Adirondack natives found employment in the barns and on the farms of the hotels and great camps.

Four

OTHER BYWAYS
HOSTELRIES

View from The Fish House, Loon Lake, Warren County, N.Y.

Fish House, with the view shown here, on Loon Lake near Chestertown in Warren County, was a little over two miles from the Riverside railroad station. It was near where the author of this book was born. E. E. Fish, the proprietor, advertised a dance pavilion nearby, good boating for fishing, fresh vegetables, milk, butter, and eggs from his farm, along with electric lights and hot and cold running water. It was located on the lake and was reached by macadam road.

On the shore of Loon Lake on the New York-Montreal Highway, Loon Lake Colony included a hotel, cottages, and a dance pavilion with a famous horseshoe bar. With 50 acres, milk and vegetables came directly from their farms. Every evening they danced to a seven-piece college orchestra. Accommodating 140 guests, they offered tennis, archery, bowling, shuffleboard, basketball, baseball, handball, horseshoes, Ping-Pong, saddle horses, boating, bathing, fishing, and free bus service. Mrs. Lester Pettigrew, proprietress, maintained that their "table was an important feature." Loon Lake, one of the two Loon Lakes in the Adirondacks, was on the eastern Adirondacks today's Route 9. After working at the 1932 Olympics, the author's father, Ross Williams, opened a Socony Station about a half mile from the Loon Lake Colony.

The Palisades on the west shore of Brant Lake was in "lake" country. They were 8 miles from Schroon Lake, 11 miles from Friends and Loon Lakes, and 16 miles from Lake George. The hotel accommodated 125 for fishing, hunting, swimming, boating, and riding saddle horses. The proprietor J. C. Bacon arranged auto stage transportation from the Riverside railroad station, 14 miles away. William Owens and J. C. Bacon were early proprietors.

Grove Point House, Schroon Lake, Adirondack Mts. N. Y.

The Grove Point House, located about a half mile south of Schroon Lake Village, was a regular stop on the steamboat route. It prospered as an Adirondack hostelry because its manager, Capt. W. A. Mackenzie, was known to be thorough, energetic, and obliging. The 75-guest hotel was equipped with modern conveniences, including electric bulbs. Note the octagon tower on top of the house providing a view of the lake and surrounding mountains.

Mc.Phillips 's Hotel, Friends Lake, Adirondack Mts.

The McPhillips brothers opened their hostelry, overlooking Friends Lake, one of six on the lake, two miles from the train station in "one of the most beautiful locations in the Adirondack Mountains." The lake was stocked with the best of bass, perch, pike, and other freshwater fish. In 1924, they advertised a "long distance telephone connection." The McPhillips brothers also offered desirable campsites for sale on the west shore of Friends Lake.

845 OTTER LAKE HOTEL, OTTER LAKE, N. Y. ADIRONDACK MTS.

The Otter Lake Hotel was pleasantly situated on Otter Lake, 42 miles from Utica. The 100-guest hotel was seasonal, open June 15 to September 15. Guests paid from $10 to $20 per week with daily rates $2–$3. In the promotional publications of the early 1900s, the Otter Lake Hotel was listed as a first-class hotel in every respect where patrons were assured of courteous treatment and a delightful outing.

Forts Hotel at Caroga Lake was an imposing two-story building with porches on both levels. It was located in central Caroga Lake Village, just past Sherman's Amusement Park. Built sometime before 1910, it was there before the park. The stone foundations of the hotel's large boat dock, which was directly in front of the hotel, can still be seen in the water at the far end of Sherman's beach.

Many of the Adirondack hotels promoted their offerings with a "free from hay fever" claim. The Canada Lake Hotel, built in the late 1880s by James Fulton, added the health advantage along with several boating opportunities on Canada Lake. Those traveling to the hotel in the first decade of the 1900s rode the horse-drawn Canada Lake Stage where one rider reported the four-hour ride "was no picnic." Again, in October 1914, another popular Adirondack hotel succumbed to fire.

Mountain Lake, 200 feet above sea level, was reached by an electric trolley line from Gloversville. In 1900, Elmer Hilts took over the 1890s Mountain Lake Hotel and gave it the Mountain Lake name. Tragedy came to the resort shortly after 3:00 a.m. on the morning of August 4, 1908, when a severe thunderstorm set the Mountain Lake Hotel on fire. It was discovered by Mrs. George Sowle, wife of the proprietor, who awakened all the guests and got them out safely.

Frank Maxam was one of the first to offer cottage accommodations in Warren County. His camps and cottages on Garnet Lake, 13 miles from the railroad station at Riverside, accommodated 20. During the June to November season, terms were $10 per week at "a place that's different." The bungalows at Maxam's Camp were constructed with vertical logs, a practice followed in other Adirondack locales. When the logs were split in half to form a flat wall inside, the building could be built with half the number of logs.

Cameron's Lodge, Athol, N.Y.   Pub. by Don. H. Cameron,

Don H. Cameron's Farmhouse and Lodge at Athol in Warren County accommodated 60 guests with Rexford C. Reynolds as proprietor. Before the days of large hotels, many Adirondack farmhouses became the first hostelries, offering accommodations for the visitors, including the sportsmen who came to hunt and fish in the woods and lakes. Farm children often gave up their beds for paying guests and slept under the dining room table or in the barn during the busy season.

BALFOUR LAKE LODGE, MINERVA, N. Y.

Minerva in the southwest corner of Essex County has a long history. Incorporated in 1817 with over 300 residents, it is almost isolated from other Adirondack settlements by the surrounding mountains. On the highway from North Creek to Newcomb, Balfour Lake was a logical place to provide a stopping-off place. Balfour Lake Lodge provided accommodations for those who found their way into the remote Adirondacks. Minerva is especially scenic during the fall foliage season.

Ye Wayside Inn, Lake Luzerne, N. Y.

Ye Wayside Inn on Lake Luzerne advertised "an unsurpassed location, in a sandy, piney region, entirely free from miasma or malaria." The 50-acre site on the shore of the lake offered bathing, fishing, walks in the woods, and "charming rest rooms." George W. LaSalle, proprietor, guaranteed "a little better beds and fresh food from the Wayside farm." P. P. Strang was an earlier owner of the inn.

Lake Luzerne Inn was a five-minute walk from the Hadley railroad station on the shore of Lake Luzerne. R. F. Tigani and G. M. Priore, managers, offered special rates for families with children at half off the $35 weekly rate. The inn accommodated 50 and served genuine French and Italian American cooking. Much like many Adirondack inns, the open season ran from June to October. Patrons were attracted by tennis, canoeing, hunting, fishing, music, and dancing.

Rockwell's hotel was located on the Upper Hudson River just above its junction with the Sacandaga River at Luzerne. It became a noted resort for sports as the junior Rockwell was one of the most successful hunters in the country. Accommodations in the original hotel, two cottages, and a 30-room annex with a grand broad piazza totaled 150. Guests arrived at the G. T. Rockwell and Son Hotel by train from Saratoga. It burned down in an 1891 fire and was rebuilt.

Adirondack Mts., N.Y., The Straight House, North Creek.

The Straight House in North Creek was not written up in *The Adirondacks* by Seneca Ray Stoddard; *Possons' Guide to Lake George, Lake Champlain, and Adirondacks* by Charles H. Possons, publisher; or other guidebooks of that day. It was off the main Adirondack trail at that time and missed the attention of the publishers. The two-story edifice appears to be typical of many of the Adirondack hostelries that took care of the traveling public from lumberjacks to the rich and famous. Robson and Abee, postcard publishers from Saratoga Springs, promoted the Straight House with colored cards printed in Germany.

Lake Harris House and Lake Harris, Newcomb, N. Y.,
"In the Adirondacks."

At Newcomb, on the state highway, a shortcut over the Adirondack watershed to Saranac Lake, Lake Placid, Paul Smiths, Malone, and beyond, was the Lake Harris House. Accommodating 75, rooms were priced at $5 per day in 1924. The three-story building was surrounded by a 10-foot piazza. It had piped in pure mountain springwater and had two good water wells on the property. It was lighted by acetylene gas. It is closed today.

HOTEL WAYSIDE, NEWCOMB, N. Y.   100120

At Newcomb, three miles from Lake Harris on the outlet of Rich Lake, was the Wayside Inn, advertised as "a large, pleasant, and comfortable tourists' home." The owner of the Wayside Inn, John Anderson Jr., also owned the Lake Harris House and the 6,000 acres of the wild land that surrounded them. The garage in connection with the hotel had supplies and skilled mechanics in attendance. The Wayside Inn was three stories high and 200 feet long with a 12-foot, double-decked piazza.

A 1908 postcard sent from the Hotel Sherman at Moriah in Essex County tells a story repeated, time and again by those who vacation in the Adirondacks. The writer explains it this way: "We like it here very much. The Hotel Sherman is the finest we ever found in the mountains." The photograph adds to the story; the neat, imposing structure with a second-floor porch, the well-dressed patrons on the porch, and the horse-drawn carriage for transportation complete the picture of a fine hostelry in the Adirondacks.

Mary and Fred Chase, hotel workers, came from Vermont in 1878 and built a log hotel on Loon Lake in the western Adirondacks. Later it became a 500-guest hotel with cottages leading to the development of Loon Lake as a major Adirondack resort town. A nearby boardinghouse became known as the "presidents' house" because of the presidents of the United States who came as guests. Presidents Benjamin Harrison, Grover Cleveland, and William McKinley all vacationed at Loon Lake.

811 LAKE BRANTINGHAM INN, BRANTINGHAM, N. Y., ADIRONDACK MTS.

Brantingham was somewhat off the beaten track, east of Route 12 in the western Adirondack Lewis County. Surrounded by wilderness, it became a prime location for large hostelries. The Lake Brantingham Inn along with the Long Point Inn supplied rooms for those vacationing on the shores of Brantingham Lake. Some of the old Adirondack hotels later became clubhouses for private groups who wanted exclusive use of Adirondack country. In 1921, one of the old Brantingham hotels became the Wilderness Club with accommodations for families. A nine-hole golf course and a boathouse were included along with the option of building one's own camp. The property soon evolved into a real estate development to sell camps around the lake.

815 GENERAL VIEW LONG POINT INN, BRANTINGHAM, N. Y., ADIRONDACK MTS.

Hill Crest SANTA CLARA N.Y.

When Prohibition ended in 1919, Ferris Meigs, owner of the Santa Clara Lumber Company, wrote that Santa Clara "was in many respects a typical frontier town except that, as all of the property owned by the lumber company, drinking places were prohibited." Hill Crest was typical of the small hostelries that appeared on the Adirondack scene to provide accommodations for the loggers, businessmen, and tourists who found the remote Adirondack settlements and needed a place to stay.

A. A. Collins was the proprietor of the Santa Clara Lodge in the 1940s. Fishermen and hunters stayed at the lodge to take advantage of the good hunting and fishing in the northwest corner of the Adirondacks. It advertised rooms with baths. The small Log Cabin Lunch building with the gas pumps in front was being used as the post office, a welcomed addition to the small Adirondack communities as the population increased.

Star Lake in St. Lawrence County is the gateway to the northwest corner of the Adirondacks. The photograph of Star Lake Inn was published by the gift shop of G. C. Marshall. Today Star Lake is in need of an Adirondack hostelry, perhaps another Star Lake Inn. The inn advertised good boating, splendid fishing, grand scenery, quick relief from hay fever, electric lights, open fireplaces, fine orchestra, telephone stations, and accommodations for 250. Inglehart and Brown were the proprietors in 1900.

In 1892, the new house, the Rouisseaumont, opened on the high ground between Mirror Lake and Lake Placid, with a view of both. The 150-guest hotel was built and furnished to be one of the most complete and comfortable hotels in the Adirondacks. T. Edmund Krumbholz came from the Hotel Wawbeek to manage the stately hostelry. It offered golf, boating, bathing, and other usual offerings of the hotels, and it was known as a "homelike mountain retreat." Rates were $4 per day in 1900.

New Watch Rock Hotel from Schroon Lake, Adirondack, N. Y.

The 1924 publicity booklet by the Delaware and Hudson Railroad, *A Summer Paradise*, promoted the Watch Rock Hotel. According to the booklet, the 129-guest Watch Rock Hotel and Cottages was a "modern house with sanitary plumbing" on Schroon Lake. It had its own gas plant and electric lights. The piazza was 30 feet wide and 200 feet long. They offered "beautiful grounds, plenty of shade, no mosquitoes or malaria, air dry and healthful, nights always cool." Baseball and mountain climbing were popular pastimes at the resort. In the 1920s, the Watch Rock Hotel and the Rising House in Chestertown were under the same management with John O'Connell in charge. An earlier proprietor, George Cecil, offered "an excellent table and a house with nice and wholesome character." When J. D. Benham was manager he sent out booklets and diagrams to prospective guests. His "mountain paradise" offered the first rent-a-car in the Adirondacks as early as 1912. The lake steamers on Schroon Lake stopped at the dock six times a day. The main building was surrounded by cottages, some occupied by owners and others part of the hotel business.

The Leland House at Schroon Lake welcomed guests from 1872 to 1950. J. Monroe Leland and his two sons, William G. and C. Thurman, were the founders of Schroon Lake's largest hotel. The original 125-guest Leland House building was three stories high with a two-story porch facing the lake. It had a 107-foot-high observatory on the roof. The structure was enlarged and improved through the 1870s. In 1886, Lorenzo and Elmore Locke took control of the Leland House and added flush toilets. They enlarged the dining room to 300 seats and built a separate dining room for children and maids. The Locke brothers died unexpectedly in 1894 of consumption, and the mortgage holders, Effingham P. Nichols and Francis Dana, took the house. They sold the business to Louis W. Emerson and his brother James, with Thurman Leland staying on as manager. As a state senator, James Emerson succeeded in getting paved roads to Schroon Lake, opening it up for increased tourist trade. On Halloween night in 1914, a cigar tossed into a pile of leaves caused a fire that burned down the big hotel. A new Colonial-style hotel was built for the 1915 season, replacing the original Victorian-style Leland House.

The Ondawa House on Schroon Lake offered special terms for families in its 100-guest hotel. Patrons could take the train to Riverside and then be transported by stage or autobus the 17 miles to the house. It was operated by Paris Russell and John Conley on the site of an earlier hotel in 1862. John Burwell was the manager for many years and was succeeded by Frank Bailey. The 300 feet of veranda looked out on the park, the lawns, the croquet grounds, and a playground.

SCHROON LAKE
MANOR HOUSE
GOLF COU
7 T.
MANOR
ANNEX
6
AKESIDE BOAT HOUSE
CADDY HOUSE
1 T.
VEGETABLES
PUTTING
GREEN
DRIVING
NETS
BOAT HOUSE
BASE BALL
TENNIS
HAND BALL
BOATS
STAGE
1C
CRIB
TENNIS
IVING
ROLLER
SKATING
ROPES
BEACH

In the Manor of Scaroon . . . From the day when it first opened, Scaroon has skillfully blended its lavish hospitality, excellent accommodations and gracious service, into a vacation wonderland of charm and prestige unsurpassed. Catering to an enviable clientele of adult young people, who appreciate and demand the best, informality and friendliness have always reigned supreme. It's "hi neighbor" from the first cheery "hello" to the last

Here truly you'll find that "Hearts are Happ Taut nerves relax, tension recedes and living i Manor of Scaroon becomes again, a really ple able art. You'll relish every moment of your

SCAROO

In February 1969, there was a big fire in northern Warren County; the once famous resort the 250-guest Scaroon Manor was leveled by a deliberate fire. New York State took ownership of the 450-acre property in 1967 to establish a new state campground with a public beach on Schroon Lake. It had an auction to sell off the buildings. Of these buildings, 41 were sold and over 30 had to be burned. Joseph Frieber was a longtime, well-known manager of the Scaroon

Labels visible on the illustration: U.S. HIGHWAY #9, SPRING, SPRING HOUSE, SADDLE HORSES, MAIN HOUSE, VEGETABLES, ICE, STORE, STAFF, GARAGES, PARCELL, MANOR

HARRY CHANDLER MAP

Manor complex. With its two miles of lake frontage, it was known as "the camp hotel supreme." It advertised adherence to dietary laws and had an excellent Hungarian cuisine. It was big news when the Warner Brothers Film Company came to the Adirondacks to film the movie *Marjorie Morningstar* at the Scaroon Manor. The once thriving, beautifully landscaped resort is today one of New York's newest campgrounds.

Ausable Chasm, N. Y. Hotel Ausable Chasm and Rainbow Falls.

The Hotel Ausable Chasm, located near the famous Adirondack natural attraction Ausable Chasm, was easily reached by railroad. Accommodating 200 guests, the hotel had all modern improvements, including artesian well water. An elevator served the four-story building. William P. Gardiner, manager, arranged to pick up guests from the railroad station by automobile at all trains. A large garage with supplies was connected with the hotel. Horace H. Nye became manager in the 1920s.

Hotel Champlain on Lake Champlain, N. Y.

Hotel Champlain opened in 1890 as the Bluff Point Hotel. It was "a metropolitan hotel in the summer paradise" and was also "the summer rendezvous of people of culture and refinement," according to the Delaware and Hudson 1927 booklet A Summer Paradise. The 400-by-90-foot hotel was located on Bluff Point above Lake Champlain. The golf course that was connected with the hotel was the third oldest in the United States and the first built by a resort hotel. Today the hotel serves as a community college.

114

Florence K Rennell was the proprietress of the Lakeside Inn at Port Kent in the 1920s. Earlier publications listed M. J. and F. K. Rennell, proprietors and ownership/management. Buses met the Delaware and Hudson trains at the Port Kent station and transported the guests to the 125-guest hotel. Water sports were featured along with the main ferryboat from the Adirondacks to the Green Mountains of Vermont. A new cement road led to Ausable Chasm, three miles away.

The 100-guest Northern Pines Inn claimed to be "one of the good hotels on Lake Champlain." The owner, W. H. Sussdorff, developed 1,200 acres of mountains, woods, and beachfront at Port Kent into a complete resort. The hotel offered pure springwater, a roof garden for dancing, an 18-hole golf course, tennis, a swimming pool, and fishing. J. S. Brokaw, manager, kept out "undesirable persons and those afflicted with pulmonary troubles." In the 1920s, it offered "analyzed spring water."

The Windsor, Elizabethtown, N. Y. In the Adirondacks.

Orlando Kellogg and his son were the proprietors of the Windsor and Cottages at Elizabethtown. Kellogg's automobiles and carriages met all trains and boats at Westport; the Windsor was the largest and most up-to-date hotel on the eastern side of the Adirondacks at the beginning of the 20th century. Swimmers could enjoy an open-air pool. The Windsor had a private trout pond for fishing, and it was the "earnest endeavor of the proprietors of the 250-guest hotel to make it homelike and attractive," according to Seneca Ray Stoddard's 1892 *The Adirondacks*.

The Mansion House at Elizabethtown with Simonds and Kellogg as proprietors was especially designed for summer boarders. The 200-guest hotel was located on a hill at the southern end of the village, with verandas on three sides. The building was three stories high with large, well-furnished rooms. They opened the hostelry to accommodate the growing crowds flocking to Pleasant Valley. The four-horse coach brought guests to and from the Lake Champlain steamboat landing.

E. M. Leclair was the proprietress of the Twin Elms of Upper Jay, also known as "the Heart of the Adirondacks." The business was on the state road, 16 miles southeast of Lake Placid. She offered, in 1921, ample automobile storage to meet the needs of the new automobile traffic coming to the Adirondacks. At one time, 85 guests were welcomed to her hotel and cottages at $25 per week. She advertised the location on the Albany-to-Montreal highway, which is today's Route 9N.

Summer boarders began to find their way to Stony Creek in the 20th century. Farm and village homes, such as the Perkins House, took boarders for a few weeks in the summer to add to the family income. Earlier the Perkins House had been known as the Bell Lodge. An attractive new sign was placed on the home in April 1914. Sometime later, Orrin Perkins had upgraded and repaired the hostelry and planned on constructing an addition in early summer to enlarge the house. Unfortunately, it burned before he could expand.

Elizabethtown, the county seat of Essex County, was a town without mills that produced some of the brightest legal minds of that day. With the Bouquet River running through the village and the grand panorama of surrounding lofty peaks and ranges of the Adirondacks, the setting became a natural attraction for visitors. Benjamin F. Stetson, proprietor of the Deers Head Inn, developed the business into a major attraction beginning in 1808. Accommodating 150, it was open year-round, offering such amenities as an orchestra, dancing, saddle horses,

mountain climbing, steam-heated rooms, and, later, an automobile that met all trains and boats at Westport, seven miles away. By 1939, the Deers Head Inn was under the proprietorship of Bastian and Jaeger. In the 1940s, Stella Bastian was the proprietress and E. J. Bastian was the manager. Although a portion of the complex is now gone, what remains may be the oldest inn in the Adirondacks.

The 1868 Stranahan Atlas of Montgomery and Fulton Counties places a hotel, the G. Spencer Hotel, in the heart of downtown Stratford. The New Century Atlas of Montgomery and Fulton Counties locates the L. Service Hotel on the same site in 1905. Settlers had been moving into Stratford since 1800. Farmers and tanners fed the economy of the town, and it grew, so that by the mid-1800s, the population reached 800. The surrounding lakes and forestlands attracted sportsmen and others who patronized the Service Hotel.

Alfred Dolge, a Dolgeville factory owner and developer of the Little Falls-Dolgeville Railroad, purchased 4,500 acres of Adirondack land in 1892 for a land development project. In 1897, he formed the Aukskerada Park Club and sold shares. In 1898, a bankruptcy ended his dream, and Cyrus Durey continued the development. Dolge built the Auskerada Hotel and suggested to those who rode his railroad and took the 10-mile horse-powered ride to Canada Lake, where they could board a steamer, that they stay at his hotel.

Those who leave Wells and bear right on Route 8 pass an imposing building standing virtually alone along the forested roadway. It is the one-time boardinghouse of the Morgan Lumber Company and, later, the Girard's Griffin Gorge Hunting Camp and Farm. Today it is a private hunting camp. When the tanning and lumbering village of Griffin was thriving during the 19th century, the boardinghouse was a busy place.

When railroad tycoon William Seward Webb built his Adirondack railroad to go through his property at Nehasane in the Adirondacks, he made it possible for land-locked Beaver River to maintain a major hotel. The Beaver River Hotel (at one time the Norridge) also was on the Mohawk and Malone Railroad line that later became part of the New York Central Railroad. The hotel burned down in 1907.

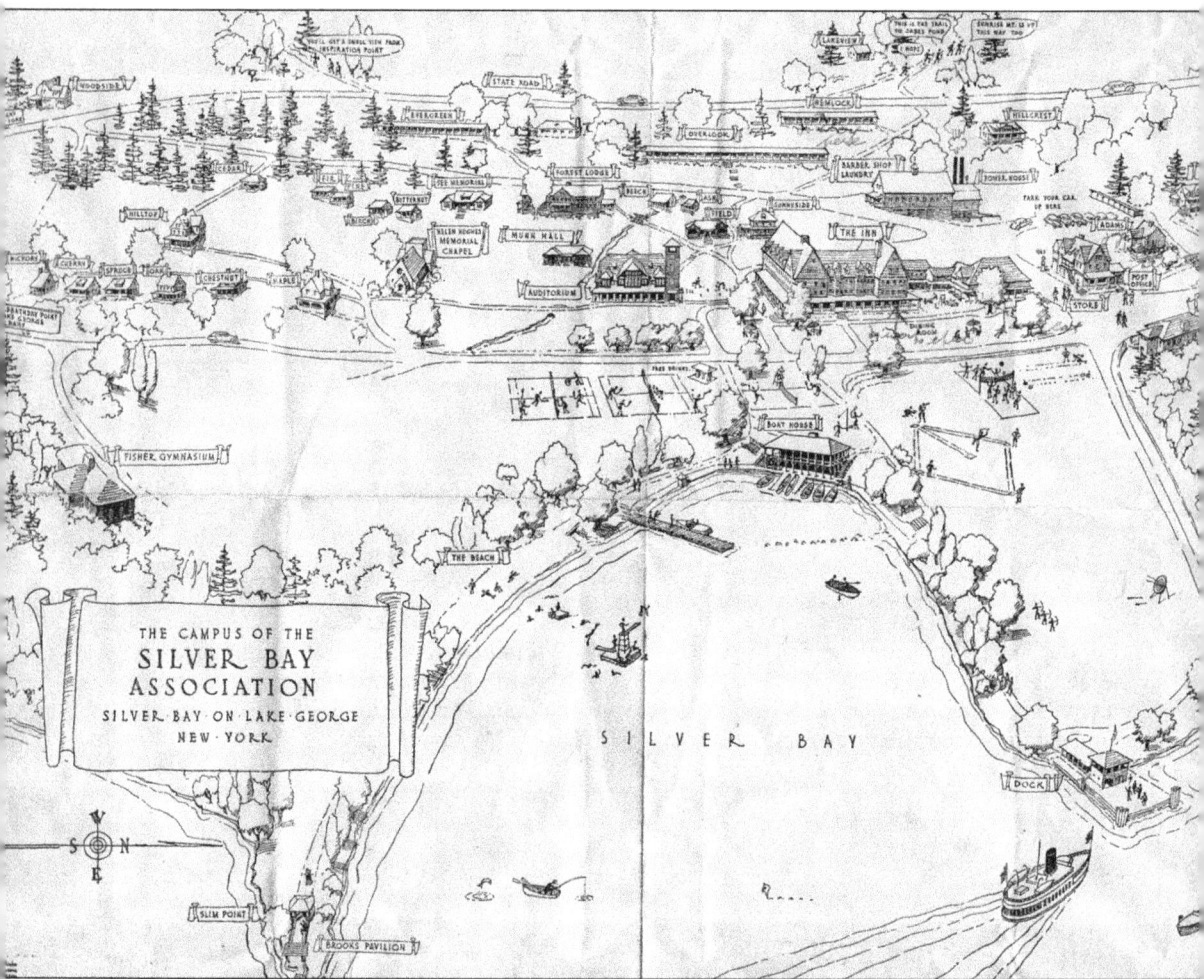

Some of the Adirondack hostelries went through an evolution from farmhouse to conference or convention center. One outstanding example is now the Silver Bay Association Christian Conference Center, owned by the YMCA on Lake George. Part of the original Ellis Patent, it was first settled by squatters in 1850. Soon it evolved into the Prouty Tourist Home, the Wilson Hotel, and then in the 1890s was developed into a hotel complex by Silas Paine, vice president of the Standard Oil Company. The hostelry was promoted as a conference center and in 1902 became a major hotel and conference center for the YMCA. Silver Bay has the capacity to host 800 guests and has a 1,000-seat auditorium. It is listed as a national historic landmark. The map of the campus shown here was drawn in 1922 by Malcolm Duncan. Note that the three dozen buildings have been named after the indigenous trees of the Adirondacks. Other buildings have been named for worthy individuals from their history.

Often the Adirondack hotels used other attractions to bring guests to the hostelries. Vroomans opened at Caroga Lake in 1907. One of the first amusement parks in the Adirondacks opened behind the hotel on the shores of Caroga Lake around 1910. Vroomans was the site of some earlier hotels, and in 1907, Edward Vrooman opened the Central Hotel, later Vroomans. In 2007, it celebrated its 100th anniversary under the proprietorship of Pat Best with her daughter Pam and son-in-law James Brockham.

Some who chose to stay in the Adirondacks built their own hostelries. Tar paper shacks provided a place to eat and sleep, and a nearby outhouse took care of the sanitary facilities. Hunting parties made good use of shacks built back in the hunting territories. They were easy to build, requiring some rough lumber, some nails, roofing paper, and possibly a small windowpane. Beds were rough bunks with hay for a mattress. Old iceboxes made good cupboards for food to keep the bears from getting it.

There was a period in the early 1800s when a majority of the hostelries were tents. Many of the later hotels and cabins evolved from tent platforms and tents. Some of the tenting facilities were quite practical with a small wood stove with a stovepipe protruding out of the canvas and with sleeping cots. Others, more elaborate, were complete with regular beds, plant stands and plants, carpets, and dressers. Some sites offered separate quarters for men or women, or for the children.

One of the main reasons for vacationing in the Adirondacks was the some 3,000 wood-ringed, clear lakes. Countless beaches, public and private, abound in Adirondack country. From the "million dollar beach" at Lake George to the old swimming hole in a forest glade, sun lovers and swimmers sought out that refreshing feeling they provided. The beach, shown here, at the head of Lake George was developed by the New York State Conservation Department in 1951. Over 100,000 swimmers use the beach each year.

The steamboats on the rivers and lakes made it possible for thousands to seek out the hostelries in the Adirondacks. The Hudson River Day Line prided itself on having the finest day passenger vessels in the country. They offered great speed, fine orchestras, spacious saloons, private parlors, and luxurious accommodations. In 1899, the *New York* and *Albany* steamers carried more than 230,000 passengers. In 1906, the *Hendrick Hudson*, 4,000 feet in length, was put into service at a cost of a million dollars. Englishman Henry Hudson explored the Hudson River for the Dutch East India Company, but his real name was Henry, not the Dutch "Hendrick," so some called the ship the "Henry Hudson." When the *New York* burned it was replaced with the *Robert Fulton* in 1909. *Washington Irving*, the largest of all, was placed into service in 1913. The steamers continued in service until 1948 after over 150 years of service.

Steamer "Albany" in the Narrows, Hudson River, N.Y.

When America's traveling public discovered the Adirondack country, transportation became a major challenge. The need to provide conveyances to get people to their Adirondack hostelries during their stay, summer and winter, provided jobs for the resident horse owners and boat owners. Here a group is off on a horse-and-wagon jaunt. Later in the season, the same horses could be pulling cutters with runners instead of wheels. Groups from the hotels would hire rigs from such livery stables as Moshers in Chestertown for a ride "around the horn." Out of Chestertown, they could go to Pottersville, Olmsteadville, Minerva, Aiden Lair, Long Lake, Tupper Lake, Blue Mountain Lake, Indian Lake, North Creek, and back through Igeona, making overnight stops on the way. Boat owners on the lakes delivered passengers and baggage to the hostelries around the lake and provided excursions through the scenic islands and surrounding woodlands circling the lake.

Much of information on Adirondack hotels and inns was gained from the thousands of postcards and photographs that were written and mailed from the Adirondack hostelries. Writing desks were another offering, often neglected, that met the needs of the patrons. Writing postcards to friends and families while on vacation in the Adirondacks was a highly popular activity, as judged by the number and variety of cards found today in family albums and by collectors and dealers. The hotel desks, often lined up along the walls of the hotel lobby or parlor, were known as writing desks or ladies' desks. The popular version of hotel desks opened in the front, creating a writing surface, and they had pigeonholes (small shelves), along with a small drawer for the writing materials. The United States Post Office Department began issuing postcards in 1873, and on May 19, 1898, Americans were authorized by an act of Congress to mail "penny postcards." In 1907, the message space was added and Adirondack vacationers could write, as one did from Blue Mountain Lake in 1923, "Am leaving here today for home. Have had a delightful time and a good rest. Plenty of water and mountains."

Visit us at
arcadiapublishing.com

www.ingramcontent.com/pod-product-compliance
Lightning Source LLC
Chambersburg PA
CBHW080545110426
42813CB00006B/1220